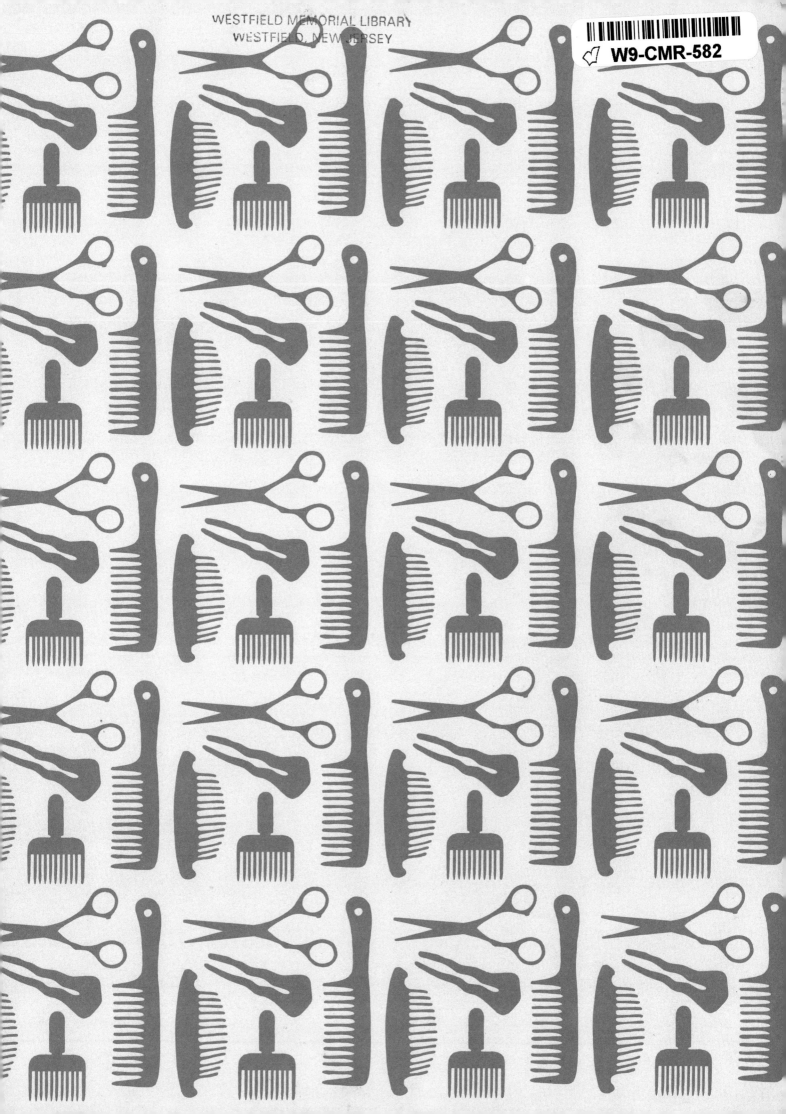

HAIRSTYLES
BRAIDING & HAIRCARE

HAIRSTYLES

BRAIDING & HAIRCARE

JACKI WADESON

Special Photography Alistair Hughes

CRESCENT BOOKS

NEW YORK • AVENEL, NEW JERSEY

This 1994 edition published by Crescent Books, distributed by
Random House Value Publishing, Inc.,
40 Engelhard Avenue, Avenel, New Jersey 07001.

Random House
New York ● Toronto ● London ● Sydney ● Auckland

© Anness Publishing Ltd 1994

1 Boundary Row
London SE1 8 HP

ISBN 0-517-10230-5

A CIP catalog record for this book is available from the Library of Congress.

Editorial Director Joanna Lorenz
Project Editor Casey Horton
Designer Ruth Prentice
Illustrator Cherril Parris

HAIR DRESSING PROJECTS
Photographer Alistair Hughes
Hair Kathleen Bray
Assisted by Wendy M B Cook
Make-up Vanessa Haines using Clinique
Models Amanda, Christiana, Carley, Laura Emily,
Frieda, Hannah, Juliet, Sarah, Zonna

Printed and bound in Singapore

ACKNOWLEDGEMENTS
Clothes from a selection at Empire; Electrical styling products from BaByliss, Braun,
Clairol, Carmen, Hair Tools, Philips, Rowenta, Vidal Sassoon; Equipment and
accessories from Celeste, Denman, Head Gardener, Kent, Jackel & Co, Laughtons, Lady
Jayne, Molton Brown; Products from Aveda, Bain de Terre, Body Shop, Citre, Clynol,
Daniel Galvin, Dome, Goldwell, John Frieda, Joico, KMS, Lamaur, Lazartigue, L'Oréal,
Matrix Essentials, Neal's Yard Remedies, Nicky Clarke, Ore-an, Paul Mitchell,
Phytologie, Poly, Redken, Revlon, Schwarzkopf, Silvikrin, St Ives, Trevor Sorbie, Wella,
Vidal Sassoon, Zotos; Wigs and hairpieces René of Paris from Trendco.

With special thanks to Richard Burns, Hairdressing Consultant.

CONTENTS

HEALTHY HAIR

BEAUTIFUL, SHINING HAIR IS A VALUABLE ASSET. IT CAN ALSO BE A VERSATILE FASHION ACCESSORY, TO BE COLORED, CURLED, DRESSED UP, OR SMOOTHED DOWN — ALL IN A MATTER OF MINUTES. HOWEVER, TOO MUCH ATTENTION COMBINED WITH THE EFFECTS OF A POOR DIET, POLLUTION, AIR-CONDITIONING, AND CENTRAL HEATING CAN MEAN THAT YOUR HAIR BECOMES THE BANE OF YOUR LIFE RATHER THAN YOUR CROWNING GLORY. A DAILY HAIRCARE ROUTINE AND PROMPT TREATMENT WHEN PROBLEMS DO ARISE ARE THEREFORE OF VITAL IMPORTANCE IN MAINTAINING THE NATURAL BEAUTY OF HEALTHY HAIR.

THE STRUCTURE OF HAIR

A human hair consists mainly of a protein called keratin. It also contains some moisture and the trace metals and minerals found in the rest of the body. The visible part of the hair, called the shaft, is composed of dead tissue: the only living part of the hair is its root, the dermal papilla, which lies snugly below the surface of the scalp in a tube-like depression known as the follicle. The dermal papilla is made up of cells that are fed by the bloodstream.

Each hair consists of three layers. The outer layer, or cuticle, is the hair's protective shield and has tiny overlapping scales, rather like tiles on a roof. When the cuticle scales lie flat and neatly overlap, the hair feels silky-soft and looks glossy. If, however, the cuticle scales have been physically or chemically damaged or broken the hair will be dull and brittle and will tangle easily.

Under the cuticle lies the cortex, which is made up of fiber-like cells that give hair its strength and elasticity. The cortex also contains the pigment called melanin, which gives hair its natural color. At the center of each hair is the medulla, consisting of very soft keratin cells interspersed with spaces. The actual function of the medulla is not known, but some authorities believe that it carries nutrients and other substances to the cortex and cuticle. This could explain why hair is affected so rapidly by changes in health.

Hair's natural shine is supplied by its own conditioner, sebum, an oil composed of waxes and fats and also containing a natural antiseptic that helps fight infection. Sebum is produced by the sebaceous glands present in the dermis. The glands are linked to the hair follicles and release sebum into them. As a lubricant sebum gives an excellent protective coating to the entire hair shaft, smoothing the cuticle scales and helping hair retain its natural moisture and elasticity. The smoother the surface of the cuticle, the more light will be reflected from the hair, and therefore the higher

HAIR STRUCTURE

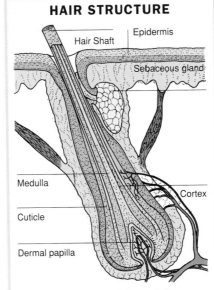

Cross-section of a human hair.

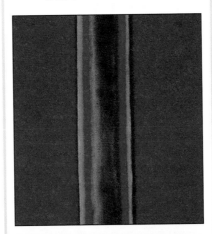

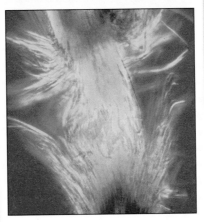

Centre and above: Pictures of a human hair magnified 200 times. A strand of hair in good condition is smooth, but if it has been damaged the outer layer is frayed and broken. Photographs courtesy of Redken Laboratories.

will be the gloss. This is why it is more difficult to obtain a sheen on curly hair than on straight hair.

Under some circumstances, for example excessive hormonal activity, the sebaceous glands produce too much sebum, and the result is oily hair. Conversely, if too little sebum is produced the hair will be dry.

THE GROWTH CYCLE

The only living part of hair is underneath the scalp – when the hair has grown through the scalp it is dead tissue. Hair goes through three stages of growth: the anagen phase when it actively grows; the catagen, or transitional phase when the hair stops growing but cellular activity continues in the papilla; and the telogen, or resting phase, when growth stops completely. During the telogen phase there is no further growth or activity at the papilla; eventually the old hair is pushed out by the new growth and the cycle begins again. The anagen phase continues for a period of two to four years, the catagen phase for only about 15-20 days, and the telogen phase for 90-120 days. At any given time, about 93 per cent of an individual's hair is in the anagen phase, 1 per cent is in the catagen phase, and 6 per cent is in the telogen phase. Scalp

FACT FILE

○ Hair grows an average of ½ in per month.
○ A single strand lives for up to seven years.
○ If a person never had their hair cut it would grow to a length of about 42 in before falling out.
○ Women have more hair than men.
○ Hair grows faster in the summer and during sleep.
○ Hair grows fastest between the ages of 16 and 24.
○ Between the ages of 40 and 50 women tend to lose about 20 per cent of their hair.
○ Hair becomes drier with age.

hair, which reacts to hormonal stimuli just like the hair on the rest of the body, is genetically programed to repeat its growth cycle 24-25 times during the average person's lifetime.

THE IMPORTANCE OF DIET

What you eat is soon reflected in the health of your hair. Like the rest of the body, healthy, shining hair depends on a good diet to ensure it is supplied with all the necessary nutrients for sustained growth and health. Regular exercise is also important as it promotes good blood circulation, which in turn ensures that vital oxygen and nutrients are transported to the hair root via the blood. Poor eating habits and lack of exercise are soon reflected in the state of the hair; even a minor case of ill-health will usually make the hair look limp and lackluster.

An adequate supply of protein in the diet is essential. Good sources include lean meat, poultry, fish, cheese, and eggs as well as nuts, seeds, and pulses. Fish, seaweed, almonds, brazil nuts, yogurt, and cottage cheese all help to give hair strength and a natural shine.

Whole grain foods and those with natural oils are highly recommended for the formation of keratin, the major component of hair. Seeds are a rich source of vitamins and minerals as well as protein. Try to eat at least three pieces of fruit a day – it is packed with fiber, vitamins, and minerals. Avoid saturated fat, which is found in red meat, fried foods, and dairy products. Choose skim or semi-skim milk rather than the whole varieties, and low-fat cheese and yogurt instead of whole cheese and cream. Substitute vegetable oils such as sunflower, safflower, and olive oil for animal fats. These foods all provide nutrients that are essential for luxuriant hair.

If you eat a balanced diet with plenty of fresh ingredients you shouldn't need to take any supplementary vitamins to promote healthy hair growth.

PROMOTING HEALTHY HAIR

○ Cut down on tea and coffee – they are powerful stimulants that act on the nervous, respiratory, and cardiovascular systems, increasing the excretion of water and important nutrients. They also hamper the absorption of minerals crucial for hair health. Drink mineral water (between six and eight glasses a day), herbal teas, and unsweetened fruit juice.

○ Alcohol dilates blood vessels and so helps increase blood flow to the tissues. However, it is antagonistic to several minerals and vitamins that are vital for healthy hair. Limit yourself to an occasional drink.

○ Regular exercise stimulates the circulatory system, encouraging a healthy blood supply to all cells and nourishing and helping to regenerate and repair.

○ Some contraceptive pills deplete the B-complex vitamins and zinc. If you notice a change in your hair after starting to take the Pill, or changing brands, ask your family doctor or nutritionist for advice.

COLOR

Hair color is closely related to skin color, which is governed by the same type of pigment, melanin. The number of melanin granules in the cortex of the hair, and the shape of the granules, determines a person's natural hair color. In the majority of cases the melanin granules are elongated in shape. People who have a large number of elongated melanin granules in the cortex have black hair, those with slightly fewer elongated granules have brown hair, and people with even less will be blonde. In other people the melanin granules are spherical or oval in shape rather than elongated, and this makes the hair appear red.

Spherical or oval granules some-times appear in combination with a moderate amount of the elongated ones, and then the person will have rich, red-dish brown tinges. If, however, spherical granules occur in combination with a large number of elongated granules then the blackness of the hair will almost mask the redness, although it will still be present to give a subtle tinge to the hair and differentiate it from pure black.

Hair color darkens with age, but at some stage in the middle years of life the pigment formation slows down and sil-very-gray hairs begin to appear. Gradually, the production of melanin ceases, and all the hair becomes colorless – or what is generally termed gray.

When melanin granules are com-pletely lacking from birth, as in albinos, the hair is pure white.

Hair color is determined by the amount of pigment in the hair and the shape of the pigment granules. People with dark hair have a larger amount of pigment than people with blonde hair. In both brunettes and blondes the pigment granules are elongated in shape: red hair results from the presence of oval-shaped granules. Photograph courtesy of Silvikrin.

Right: Red hair looks attractive whether it is worn smooth or curly. To create movement in longer hair, mist with styling lotion and set on soft rollers. If each strand of hair is twisted before winding, you will achieve a more fulsome curl. Thick, straight hair can be left to dry naturally and just finished with a shine serum. By Patrick Cameron at Alan Paul.

Below left: Brunettes look good with precision bobs that are cut to increase volume in the hair. By Yosh Toya, Photography Gen.

Below right: This naturally curly blonde hair has been quickly styled by scrunch-drying to achieve maximum volume. By Nicky Clarke, Photography Paul Cox.

STRANGE BELIEFS

The Ancient Greeks regarded blonde as the hair color of gods and heroes, but they viewed people with red hair with suspicion, and believed that strangers, rogues, and redheads should be treated with contempt. The idea that redheads were untrustworthy, deceitful, and quick-tempered was widespread in many cultures. In the Christian tradition Judas, who betrayed Christ, was said to have red hair, and artists of the early Christian period and beyond portrayed him as a redhead.

TEXTURE AND TYPE

Hair with a very curly texture needs intensive moisturizing treatments to keep the spring in the curl. On this type of hair always use a wide-toothed comb, never a brush, which will make the hair frizz. Leave-in conditioners are good for curly hair as they help to give curl separation. To revitalize curls mist with water and scrunch with the hands.

ETHNIC DIFFERENCES

Scandinavians normally have thin, straight, baby-fine hair, and mid-Europeans hair that is neither too fine nor too coarse. People native to the Indian subcontinent have coarse textured tresses while Middle Eastern populations have strong hair. In general the further east you travel the coarser hair becomes.
The hair of Chinese and Japanese people is very straight; that of Latin-speaking and North African peoples can be very frizzy and thick.

FACT FILE

○ Healthy hair is highly elastic and can stretch 20 or 30 per cent before snapping.
○ Chinese circus acrobats have been known to perform tricks while suspended by their hair.
○ A human hair is stronger than copper wire of the same thickness.
○ The combined strength of a headful of human hair is capable of supporting a weight equivalent to that of 99 people.

The texture of your hair is determined by the size and shape of the hair follicle, which is a genetic trait controlled by hormones and related to age and racial characteristics.

Whether hair is curly, wavy, or straight depends on two things: its shape as it grows out of the follicle and the distribution of keratin-producing cells at the roots. When viewed in cross section, straight hair tends to be round, wavy hair tends to be oval, and curly hair kidney-shaped. Straight hair is formed by roots that produce the same number of keratin cells all around the follicle. In curly hair however the production of keratin cells is uneven, so that at any given time there are more cells on one side of the oval-shaped follicle than on the other. Furthermore, the production of excess cells alternates between the sides. This causes the developing hair to grow first in one direction and then in the other. The result is curly hair.

The natural color of the hair also affects the texture. Natural blondes have finer hair than brunettes while redheads have the thickest hair.

Generally speaking, hair can be divided into three categories: fine, medium, and coarse and thick. Fine hair can be strong or weak; however, because of its texture, all fine hair has the same characteristic – it lacks volume. As the name suggests, medium hair is neither too thick nor too thin, and is strong and elastic. Thick and coarse hair is abundant and heavy, with a tendency to grow outwards from the scalp as well as downwards. It often lacks elasticity and is frizzy.

A single head of hair may consist of several different textures. For example, fine hair is often found on the temples, and the hairline at the front and on the nape of the head, while the texture over the rest of the head may be medium or even coarse.

NORMAL, DRY, OR OILY?

Hair type is determined by the hair's natural condition – that is, by the amount of sebum the body produces. Treatment programs such as perming, coloring, and heat styling will also have an effect on hair type. Natural hair types and those produced by applying various treatments are described below, together with advice on haircare where appropriate.

Dry hair looks dull, feels dry, tangles easily, and is difficult to comb or brush, particularly when it is wet. It is often

Thick straight hair can be made sleeker if you remember to always blow-dry downwards, which encourages the cuticles to lie flat and reflect the light. Photography courtesy of Braun.

Fine hair needs expert cutting to maximize the volume. Here gel spray was used to give lift at the roots and the hair was then blow-dried. By Taylor Ferguson.

Normal hair responds well to regular brushing, smoothing, and polishing. By Antoinette Beenders at Trevor Sorbie, for Denman, Photography Simon Bottomley.

quite thick at the roots but thinner, and sometimes split, at the ends.

Causes Excessive shampooing, over-use of heat-styling equipment, misuse of colour or perms, damage from the sun, or harsh weather conditions. Each of these factors depletes the moisture content of hair, so that it loses its elasticity, bounce, and suppleness. Dryness can also be the result of a sebum deficiency on the hair's surface, caused by a decrease in or absence of sebaceous gland secretions.

Solutions Use a nourishing shampoo and an intensive conditioner (see page 18). Allow hair to dry naturally whenever possible.

Normal hair is neither oily nor dry, has not been permed or colored, holds its style, and looks good most of the time. Normal hair is ideally suited to the daily use of two-in-one conditioning shampoos. These are formulated to provide a two-stage process in one application. When the product is lathered into wet hair the shampoo removes dirt, grease, and styling products. At this stage the

conditioner remains in the lather. As the hair is rinsed with more water, the grease and dirt are washed away. At the same time, the micro-fine conditioning droplets are released on to the hair leaving it shiny and easy to comb.

Oily hair looks lank and greasy and needs frequent washing.

Causes Overproduction of sebum as a result of hormone disturbances, stress, hot, humid atmosphere, excessive brushing, or constantly running hands through the hair, perspiration, or a diet rich in saturated fat. The hair becomes oily, sticky, and unmanageable in just a few days, or sometimes within hours.

Solutions Use a gentle, non-aggressive shampoo that also gives the hair volume. A light perm will lift the hair at the roots and limit the dispersal of sebum. Rethink your diet: reduce dairy fats and greasy foods. Try to eat plenty of fresh food, and drink six to eight glasses of water every day.

Combination hair is oily at the roots but dry and sometimes split at the ends.

Causes Chemical treatments, using detergent-based shampoos too frequently, overexposure to sunlight, and over-use of heat-styling equipment. Such repeated abuse often provokes a reaction in sebum secretion at the roots and a partial alteration in the scales, which can no longer fulfil their protective role. The hair ends therefore become dry.

Solutions Use products that have only a gentle action on the hair. Excessive use of formulations for oily hair and those for dry hair may contribute to the problem. Ideally, use a product specially designed for combination hair. If this is not possible try using a shampoo for oily hair and finish by applying a conditioner only from the middle lengths to the ends of the hair.

Colored or permed hair is very often more porous than untreated hair, so it needs gentle cleansers and good conditioners. Color-care products help prevent fading by protecting the hair from damaging rays of sunlight. Specialty products for permed hair help maintain elasticity, giving longer-lasting results.

THE CUT

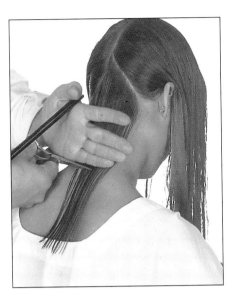

Before she had her hair cut, our model's long hair had natural movement but the weight was pulling the hair down and spoiling the shape. For her new style she wanted a shorter, more sophisticated look, and one that would be easy to maintain.

First the model's hair was shampooed, conditioned, and then combed through to remove any tangles. The stylist was then ready to start cutting. He began by sectioning off the front hair so that the hair at the back could be cut to the required length.

Next the front hair was combed forward and cut straight across at an angle. This ensured that when the model's hair was dry it would fall easily into shape.

Hair growth varies over different parts of the head. This is why your cut can appear to be out of shape very quickly. As a general rule, a short precision cut needs trimming every four weeks, a longer style every six to eight weeks. Even if you want to grow your hair long it is essential to have it trimmed regularly – at least every three months – to prevent splitting and keep the ends even.

Hairdressers use a variety of techniques and tools to make hair appear thicker, fuller, straighter, or curlier, whatever the desired effect. The techniques and tools they use are explained below.

Blunt cutting, in which the ends are cut straight across, is often used for hair of one length. The weight and fullness of the hair is distributed around the perimeter of the shape.

Clippers are used for close-cut styles and sometimes to finish off a cut. Shaved clipper cuts are popular with teenagers.

This heavily layered, graduated bob was cut close into the nape, and then the shape of the hair was emphasized by using a vegetable color to give tone and shine. The hair was styled by blow-drying. By Trevor Sorbie.

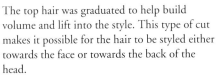

The top hair was graduated to help build volume and lift into the style. This type of cut makes it possible for the hair to be styled either towards the face or towards the back of the head.

To finish, the stylist scrunched the hair, using a blow-dryer and some mousse to encourage the formation of curls. On this type of style a diffuser fitted to the dryer will spread the airflow and give added movement to the hair. By Carlos Galico, Madrid.

Scissors can be used to reduce the bulk in thick hair. Scissors by Wella Tondeo.

Graduated hair is cut at an angle to give fullness on top and blend the top hair into shorter lengths at the nape.

Layering the hair evenly distributes the weight and fullness, giving a round appearance to the style.

Slide cutting (also called slithering or feathering) thins the hair. Scissors are used in a sliding action, backwards and forwards along the hair length. This technique is often done when the hair is dry.

Razor cutting creates softness, tapering, and internal movement so that the hair moves more freely. It can also be used to shorten hair.

Thinning, either with thinning scissors or a razor, removes bulk and weight without affecting the overall length of the hair.

CLEVER CUTS

Fine, thin, flyaway hair can be given volume, bounce, and movement by blunt cutting. Mid-length hair can benefit from being lightly layered to give extra volume, while short, thin hair can be blunt cut and the edges graduated to give movement.

Some hairdressers razor cut fine hair to give a thicker and more voluminous effect. It is best not to let fine hair grow too long. As soon as it reaches the shoulders it tends to look wispy.

Thick and coarse hair can be controlled by reducing the weight to give more style and direction. Avoid very short styles because the hair will tend to stick out. Try a layered cut with movement.

Layering also helps achieve height and eliminate weight. On shorter styles the weight can be reduced with thinning scissors expertly used on the ends only.

Sometimes hair grows in different directions, which may cause styling problems. For example, a cowlick is normally found on the front hairline and occurs when the hair grows in a swirl, backwards and then forwards. Clever cutting can redistribute the weight and go some way to solving this problem. A double crown occurs when there are two pivots for natural hair at the top of the head, rather than the usual one. Styles with height at the crown are most suitable here.

To maximize the effect of a widow's peak the hair should be taken in the reverse direction to the growth. This gives the impression of a natural wave.

For this style the model's straight hair was cut so that it would swing back into shape with every movement of the head. The shine was improved by using a longer-lasting semi-permanent color. By L'Oréal.

SHAMPOOING

Shampoos are designed to cleanse the hair and scalp, removing dirt and grime without stripping away too much of the natural sebum. They contain cleansing agents, perfume, preservatives, and conditioning agents that can coat the hair shaft to make the hair appear thicker. The conditioning agents smooth the cuticle scales so the hair doesn't tangle, and help eliminate static electricity from the hair when it dries.

THE pH FACTOR

The letters pH refer to the acid/alkaline level of a substance. It is calculated on a scale of 1 to 14. Numbers below 7 denote acidity, those over 7 alkalinity. Most shampoos range between a pH factor of 5 and 7; medicated varieties have a pH of about 7.3, which is near neutral.

Sebum has a pH factor of between 4.5 and 5.5, which is mildly acidic. Bacteria cannot survive in this pH, so it is important to maintain this protective layer in order to keep the skin, scalp, and hair in optimum condition.

Many shampoos are labelled "pH balanced", and this means they have the

Shampoos are available in different formulas to suit all hair types and conditions. Make sure you choose one that is right for your hair and use it as often as necessary to keep your hair clean. Rinse out the shampoo thoroughly. Photograph courtesy of Silvikrin.

SHAMPOO TIPS

❍ Use the correct shampoo (and not too much) for your hair type. If in doubt use the mildest shampoo you can buy.
❍ Don't wash your hair in washing-up liquid, soap, or other detergents; they are highly alkaline and will upset your hair's natural pH balance by stripping out the natural oils.
❍ Read the instructions first. Some shampoos need to be left on the scalp for a few minutes before rinsing.
❍ If you can, buy small packets of shampoo to test which brand is most suitable for your hair.

❍ Never wash your hair in the bath; dirty bath water is not conducive to clean hair, and it is difficult to rinse properly without a shower attachment or separate pourer.

❍ Always wash your brush and comb when you shampoo your hair.
❍ Change your shampoo every now and then; hair seems to develop a resistance to certain ingredients after a period of time.
❍ Don't throw away a shampoo that doesn't lather. The amount of suds are determined by the active level of detergent. Some shampoos have less suds than others but this has no effect on their cleansing ability. In fact, quite often, the more effective the product, the fewer the bubbles.

same acidity level as hair. Individuals with fragile, permed, or colored hair should use a shampoo of this type. However, for strong hair in good condition a pH balanced shampoo is unnecessary, provided shampooing is followed by conditioning.

SHAMPOO SUCCESS

Always use a product formulated for your hair type – dry, normal, oily, or chemically treated – and before shampooing brush your hair to free any tangles and loosen dirt and dead skin cells. Use lukewarm water, as hot water can be uncomfortable.

Wet the hair, then apply a small amount of shampoo and gently massage into the roots, using the pads of your fingertips; never use your nails. Pay special attention to the hairline area, places where make-up and dirt become trapped. Allow the lather to work its way to the ends of the hair. Don't rub vigorously or you will stretch the hair.

When you have finished shampooing rinse thoroughly until the water runs clean and clear. Repeat the process only if you think your hair needs it, again using only a small amount of shampoo. Finally, blot the hair with a towel to remove excess water before applying conditioner.

MASSAGING THE SCALP

Massage helps maintain a healthy scalp. It brings extra blood to the tissues, which enhances the delivery of nutrients and oxygen to the hair follicle. It also reduces scalp tension – which can contribute to hair loss – loosens dead skin cells, and helps redress the overproduction of sebum, which makes hair oily.

You can give yourself a scalp massage at home. Use warm olive oil if the scalp is dry or tight. Try equal parts of witch hazel and mineral water if you have an oily scalp. For a normal scalp, use equal parts rose and mineral waters.

Begin the massage by gently rotating your scalp using the tips of your fin-

A head massage reduces scalp tension as well as promoting healthy hair growth. It is also a relaxing and pampering treatment that you can do yourself at home.

gers. Start at the forehead, move to the sides, and work over the crown to the nape of the neck. Then place your fingertips firmly on the scalp without exerting too much pressure. Push the fingers together then pull them apart through the hair in a kneading motion, without lifting or moving them. When you have massaged for about a minute, move to the next section. Continue until your entire scalp and upper neck have been treated.

ELABORATE HAIR STYLES

In the 17th and 18th centuries hair washing was a biennial event. Fashionable women contrived towering heads of hair adorned with vegetables, fruit, feathers, and even vases of flowers. Many ladies sat up all night dozing in chairs rather than spoil their head pieces by lying in bed.

GETTING INTO CONDITION

Long hair needs a regular conditioning regime to keep it healthy and shiny. By Daniel Galvin, for L'Oréal Coiffure, Photography Iain Philpott.

In an ideal world a regular shampoo would be sufficient to guarantee a glossy head of hair. Unfortunately very few people are able to wash their hair and let the matter rest at that; most need some sort of help just to overcome the effects of modern living, not to mention the occasional problem that needs treatment. Here is a guide to the vast array of products available to get the hair in excellent condition.

THE CONDITIONERS

Glossy hair has cuticle scales that lie flat and neatly overlap, thus reflecting the light. Perming and coloring, rough handling, and heat styling all conspire to lift the cuticles, allowing moisture to be lost from the cortex and making hair dry, lackluster, and prone to tangle. Severely damaged cuticles break off completely, which means that the hair gets thinner and eventually breaks.

To put the shine back into hair and restore its natural luster it may be necessary to use a specific conditioner that meets the hair's requirements. Conditioners, with the exception of hot oils, should be applied to freshly shampooed hair that has been blotted dry with a towel to remove excess moisture.

Today there is a large, and sometimes confusing, number of conditioners on the market. The following list describes those which are widely available.

Basic conditioners coat the hair with a fine film, temporarily smoothing down the cuticle and making hair glossier and easier to manage. Leave for a few minutes before rinsing thoroughly.

Conditioning sprays are used prior to styling and form a protective barrier against the harmful effects of heat. They are also good for reducing static electricity on flyaway hair.

Hot oils give an intensive, deep nourishing treatment. To use, place the unopened tube in a cup of hot tap water and leave to heat for one minute. Next, wet the hair and towel it dry before twisting off the tube top. Massage the hot oil evenly into the scalp and throughout the hair for one to three minutes. For a more intensive treatment cover the head with a shower cap. To finish, rinse the hair and shampoo.

Intensive conditioners help hair to retain its natural moisture balance, replenishing it where necessary. Use this type if the hair is split, dry, frizzy, or difficult to manage. Distribute the conditioner evenly through the hair and then allow it to penetrate for two to five minutes, or longer if required. Rinse very thoroughly with lots of fresh water, lifting your hair from the scalp to ensure any residue is washed away.

Leave-in conditioners are designed to help retain moisture, reduce static, and add shine. They are especially good for fine hair as they avoid conditioner overload, which can cause lankness. Convenient and easy-to-use, they also provide a protective barrier against the effects of heat styling. Apply after shampooing but don't rinse off. These products are ideal for daily use.

Restructurants penetrate the cortex, helping to repair and strengthen the inner part of damaged hair. They are helpful if the hair is lank and limp and has lost its natural elasticity as a result of chemical treatments or physical damage.

Split end treatments/serums condition damaged hair. The best course of action for split ends is to have the ends trimmed, but this does not always solve the whole problem because the hair tends to break off and split at different levels. As an intermediate solution, split ends can be temporarily sealed using these specialized conditioners. They should be worked into the ends of newly washed hair so that they surround the hair with a microscopic film that leaves the hair shaft smoother.

Color/perm conditioners are designed for chemically treated hair. After-color products add a protective film around porous areas of the hair, preventing color loss. After-perm products help stabilize the hair, thus keeping the bounce in the curl.

PROBLEMS AND SOLUTIONS

Split ends, dandruff, and dry, itchy scalp are common problems that can detract from otherwise healthy hair. In most cases such problems can be overcome by giving the appropriate treatment.

Dandruff consists of scaly particles with an oily sheen that lie close to the hair root. This condition should not be confused with a flaky scalp (see below).

Causes Poor diet, sluggish metabolism, stress, a hormonal imbalance, and sometimes infection. These conditions produce increased cell renewal on the scalp, which is often associated with an increase in sebum. The scales will absorb the excess oil, but if the problem is untreated it will become worse.

Solutions Rethink your diet and lifestyle. Learn relaxation techniques if the problem appears to be caused by stress. Brush the hair before shampooing and scrupulously wash combs and brushes. Always choose a mild shampoo with an antidandruff action that gently loosens scales and helps prevent new ones. Follow with a treatment lotion, massaged into the scalp using the fingertips. The treatment must be used regularly if it is to be effective. Avoid excessive use of heat stylers. If the dandruff persists, consult your family doctor or trichologist.

Flaky/itchy scalp produces tiny white pieces of dead skin that flake off the scalp and are usually first noticed on the shoulders. This condition can often be confused with dandruff but the two are not related. Sometimes the scalp is red or itchy and feels tense. The hair has a dull appearance.

Causes Hereditary traits, stress, insufficient rinsing of shampoo, lack of sebum, using a harsh shampoo, vitamin imbalance, pollution, air conditioning and central heating.

Solutions Choose a moisturizing shampoo and a conditioner with herbal extracts to help soothe and remoisturize the scalp.

Leave-in conditioners that come in mousse formulations can be applied straight on to the hair from the container.

Use a styling comb with widely spaced teeth to distribute the conditioner from the roots to the ends of the hair. Do not rinse out, simply style and dry the hair as desired.

Above and right: Limp, fine hair can be transformed easily using a volumizing spray or thickening mousse before setting on large rollers. Make sure the hair is completely dry before removing rollers and lightly brushing the hair through. Hold with hairspray. By Nicky Clarke, Photography Paul Cox.

Fine hair tends to be limp, looks flat, and is difficult to style because it does not hold a style.

Causes The texture is hereditary, but the problem is often made worse by using too heavy a conditioner, which weighs the hair down. Excessive use of styling products can have the same effect.

Solutions Wash hair frequently with a mild cleanser and use a light conditioner. Volumizing shampoos can help give body, and soft perms will make hair appear thicker.

Frizzy hair results from the merest hint of rain or other air moisture being absorbed into the hair. It looks dry, lacks luster, and is difficult to control.

Causes Can be inherited or caused by rough treatment, such as too much harsh brushing or pulling the hair into rubber bands.

Solutions When washing the hair, massage the shampoo into the roots and allow the lather to work its way to the ends. Apply a conditioner from the mid-lengths of the hair to the ends, or use a leave-in conditioner. The hair is often best styled with a gel, which should be applied when the hair is wet. Alternatively, allow the hair to dry naturally and then style it using a wax or pomade. Serums can also help. These are silicone-based products that work by surrounding the cuticle with a transparent microscopic film, which leaves the hair shaft smoother. Serums effectively prevent moisture loss and inhibit the absorption of dampness from the surrounding air.

Split ends occur when the cuticle is damaged and the fibers of the cortex unravel. The hair is dry, brittle, and prone to tangling, and can split at the end or anywhere along the shaft.

Causes Over-perming or coloring, insufficient conditioning, or too much brushing or backcombing, especially with poor quality combs or brushes. Careless use of spiky rollers and hair pins, excessive heat styling and not having the hair trimmed regularly can also cause the problem.

Solutions Split ends can't be mended; the only long-term cure is to have them

snipped off. What is lost in the length will be gained in quality. It may help if you reduce the frequency with which you shampoo, as this in itself is stressful to hair and causes split ends to extend up the hair shaft. Never use a dryer too near the hair, or set it on too high a temperature. Minimize the use of heated appliances. Try conditioners and serums that are designed to temporarily seal split ends and give resistance to further splitting.

Product build-up is the residue of styling products and two-in-one shampoo formulation left on the hair shaft.

Causes When these residues combine with mineral deposits in the water a build-up occurs, preventing thorough cleansing and conditioning. The result is hair that is dull and lacks luster; it is often difficult to perm or color successfully because there is a barrier preventing the chemicals from penetrating the hair shaft. The color can be patchy and the perm result uneven.

Solutions Use one of the stripping, chelating or clarifying shampoos, which are specially designed to remove product build-up. This is particularly important prior to perming or coloring.

Top left and above: Frizzy hair can be controlled using a moisturizing shampoo and conditioner. Style using a mousse designed for curly hair, which will help to eliminate tangles and reduce static. Finish with a few drops of serum to add a final touch of gloss. By Nicky Clarke, Photography Paul Cox.

Above left: Split ends can't be mended, just temporarily sealed. The only permanent cure is to have your hair trimmed regularly.

Natural ingredients such as herbs and essential oils can help you achieve beautifully conditioned hair. Here a hot oil treatment was applied to the model's hair to enhance its shine and condition. Natural oils that are suitable for applying to the hair and scalp include vegetable oils, but rosemary, ylang ylang, and lavender essential oils are fragrant alternatives. Use according to the manufacturer's directions. By Daniel Galvin.

NATURAL SOLUTIONS

Since time immemorial herbs and plants have been used to heal, pamper, and beautify. Many of these age-old haircare recipes still apply today. The following are a few you might like to try at home. Remember to use them immediately after you have made them: they won't keep.

Dandruff solution

Mix a few drops of oil of rosemary with 2 tbsp of olive oil and rub well into the scalp at bedtime. Shampoo and rinse thoroughly in the morning.

Egg shampoo

In a blender mix together two small eggs with ¼ cup of still mineral water and 1 tbsp of cider vinegar or lemon juice. Blend for 30 seconds at low speed. Massage well into the scalp and rinse very thoroughly using lukewarm water (if the water is any hotter the egg will begin to set).

Herbal shampoo

Crush a few dried bay leaves with a rolling pin and mix with a handful of dried camomile flowers and one of rosemary. Place in a large jug and pour over 3½ cups of boiling water. Strain after 2-3 minutes and mix in 1 tsp of soft or liquid soap. Apply to the hair, massaging well. Rinse thoroughly.

Hot oil

Any vegetable oil is suitable for conditioning. Just heat the oil until slightly warm. Rub a little into your scalp and then through every part of your hair, massaging gently as you go. Cover your head with a plastic shower cap for 20 minutes; the heat from your head will help the oil penetrate the hair shaft. Shampoo and rinse thoroughly.

Intensive conditioning treatment

Warm 1 tbsp each of wheat germ and olive oil and massage gently into the scalp. Wrap a warm towel around the head and leave for 10 minutes. Then rinse with a basin of water to which you have added the juice of a lemon.

Hair tonic

Beat ⅔ cup of natural yogurt with an egg; add 1 tsp of sea kelp powder and 1 tsp of finely grated lemon rind. Mix thoroughly and work into the hair. Cover your hair with a plastic shower cap and leave in place for 40 minutes. Shampoo and rinse.

Using essential oils

Pure aromatherapy oils can be used for hair care. The following recipes come from world-famous aromatherapist Robert Tisserand. The number of drops of oil, as listed, should be diluted in 2 tbsp of vegetable oil, which will act as a carrier oil.

Dry hair: rosewood 9, sandalwood 6.
Oily hair: bergamot 9, lavender 6.
Dandruff: eucalyptus 9, rosemary 6.

Mix the required treatment and apply to dry or wet hair. Massage the scalp using the fingertips. Leave for two to five minutes. Shampoo and rinse thoroughly.

You can grow your own herbs or find them and other ingredients such as essential oils and henna in many health food shops and pharmacies. They are also available through specialty shops selling natural remedies and beauty products. Many hair treatments can be made safely, economically, and easily at home.

HAIR RINSES

Lemon juice added to the rinsing water will brighten blonde hair, while 2 tbsp of cider vinegar will add gloss and body to any color hair.

Other rinses (to be used after shampooing) can be made up to treat a variety of hair problems. First you must make an infusion by placing 2 tbsp of the fresh herb in a china or glass bowl. Fresh herbs are best, but if you are using dried herbs remember they are stronger so you will need to halve the amount required for fresh herbs. Add 2 cups boiling water, cover and leave to steep for three hours. The longer the herbs steep the stronger the infusion. Strain before using.

Make infusions with the following herbs for the specific uses as listed:

○ Southernwood to combat grease.
○ Nettle to stimulate hair growth.
○ Rosemary to prevent static.
○ Lavender to soothe a tight scalp.

Make a parsley hair tonic (see picture right) by blending a large handful of parsley sprigs and 2 tbsp water in a food processor until well puréed. Apply to the scalp, cover with a shower cap, and leave for an hour before rinsing thoroughly.

TIMES OF CHANGE

Hair goes through many different stages during a lifetime. Each stage brings with it different requirements in haircare. The most significant stages are described below, together with recommendations for promoting hair health during each phase.

BEGINNINGS: THE BABY AND CHILD

A baby's hair characteristics are determined from the very moment of conception. By the 16th week of pregnancy the foetus will be covered with lanugo, a downy body hair that is usually shed before birth. The first hair appears on the head at around 20 weeks gestation and it is at this time that the pigment melanin, which will determine the color of the hair, is first produced.

A few weeks after birth the baby's original hair begins to fall out or is rubbed off. The new hair is quite different from the initial downy mass, so a baby born with blonde wispy curls might have dark straight hair by the age of six months.

Cradle cap, which appears as thick, yellow scales in patches over the scalp, causes many mothers concern. Cradle cap is the result of a natural build-up of skin cells. It is nothing to worry about and can be gently loosened by rubbing a little baby oil on to the scalp at night and washing it off in the morning. This may need to be repeated for several days until all the loose scales have been lifted and washed away.

Mothers often carefully trim their baby's hair as and when necessary, and it is not until the child is about two years of age that a visit to a hairdressing salon may be necessary. Children's hair is normally in beautiful condition and is best cut and styled simply.

At the onset of puberty young adults suddenly become much more interested in experimenting with their hair. This is when they may experience oily hair and skin for the first time. A re-evaluation of the shampoos and conditioners currently in use is often necessary to keep hair looking good.

HAIRCARE DURING PREGNANCY

During pregnancy the hair often looks its best. However after the birth, or after breast-feeding ceases, about 50 per cent of new mothers experience what appears to be excessive hair loss. This is related to the three stages of hair growth (see page 8). During pregnancy and breast-feeding, hormones keep the hair at the growing stage for longer than usual, so it appears thicker and fuller. Some time after the birth – usually about 12 weeks later – this hair enters the resting stage, at the end of which all the hair that has been in the resting phase is shed. What appears to have been excessive hair loss is therefore simply a postponement of a natural occurrence, a condition that is known as post-partum alopecia.

A more significant problem that may occur during pregnancy is caused by a depletion in the protein content of the hair. As a result the hair becomes drier and more brittle. Combat this by frequent use of an intensive conditioning treatment.

GROWING UP

A baby's hair is soft and downy at first but it takes on its individual characteristics within six months of birth.

The toddler's hair requires a simple cut. At this stage the child is usually taken for her first visit to a salon.

Young boys need a hair cut that is easily combed into shape. By Regis.

Bobs suit most girls and are perfect for straight hair, but need regular trims. By Regis.

Avoid perming during pregnancy because the hair is in an altered state and the result can be unpredictable. Try a herbal rinse to give your hair and your spirits a lift.

GROWING OLDER

With aging the whole body slows down, including the hair follicles, which become less efficient and produce hairs that are finer in diameter and shorter in length. Such shrinkage is gradual and the hair begins to feel slightly thinner, with less volume and density. At the same time the sebaceous glands start to produce less sebum and the hair begins to lose its color as the production of melanin decreases.

Blonde hair fades, brunettes lose their natural highlights, and redheads tone down to brownish shades. When melanin production stops altogether the new hair that grows is white, not gray as is commonly perceived. The production of melanin is governed by genetic factors, and the best indication of when an individual's hair will become white is the age at which their parents' hair lost its color. Pigment, apart from giving hair its color, also helps to soften and make each strand more flexible. This is why white hair tends to become wirier and coarser in texture.

Because the texture changes, the hair is inclined to pick up dust and smoke from the atmosphere, so it soon appears to be discolored and dirty. This is particularly true for those who live in a town or spend time in smoky atmospheres. Cigarette smoke and natural gas from cookers discolor white hair and make it look yellow. Mineral deposits from chlorinated water can give white hair a greenish tinge. Chelating, clarifying, or purifying shampoos will help to strip this build-up from the hair.

To counteract dryness associated with aging, use richer shampoos and conditioning products. As well as regular conditioning, weekly intensive treatments are essential to counteract moisture loss.

As women grow older the hair becomes thinner. A mid-length to short cut makes the hair less prone to droop. By Joseph and Jane Harling.

AS THE YEARS GO BY

Medium-textured hair that needs a lift can be given height on the crown with a root perm. By Paul Falltricks, for Clynol.

The hair has been cut to create more movement and softness. It was then scrunch-dried and finished with wax. By Regis.

Long hair was softened by feathering the sides and cutting full bangs. A semi-permanent color added gloss. By Nicky Clarke.

Fine gray hair was highlighted and then toned using a rinse before blow-drying with a round brush. By Essanelle Salons.

VACATION HAIRCARE

Permed hair needs extra protection from the drying effects of sun, salt, chlorine, and wind. Use plenty of conditioner and always rinse your hair after swimming. Curl revitalizers help by putting moisture back and keeping curls bouncy. Photograph courtesy of Bain de Terre Spa Therapy.

More damage can be done to the hair during a two-week vacation in the sun than the damage accrued during the rest of the year. The ultraviolet rays or radiation (UVRs) from sunlight that can cause damage to the skin can also have an adverse effect on the hair, depleting the natural oils and removing moisture. Strong winds whip unprotected hair into a tangle, causing breakage and split ends. Chlorinated and salt water cause color fading and result in drooping perms.

Permed and colored hair, weakened by chemicals, lose moisture at a faster rate than untreated hair. White hair is particularly susceptible to the effects of the sun because it has lost its natural pigmentation (melanin), which to some degree helps to filter out harmful UVRs.

OUT IN THE MID-DAY SUN

Protecting the hair from the sun's harmful rays makes as much sense as protecting the skin. Wear a hat or a scarf on the beach or use a sun protective spray to shield the hair from the sun's harmful rays. After a swim, rinse the salt or chlorinated water thoroughly from the hair using plenty of fresh, clean water. If fresh water is not available take some with you in an empty soft drinks bottle or use bottled water.

Sun screen gels are available for the hair and these offer a good deal of protection. Comb the gel through your hair and leave on all day. Remember to reapply the gel after swimming. Alternatively, use a leave-in conditioner, choosing one that protects the hair against UVRs.

On windy or blustery days keep long hair tied back to prevent tangles. Long hair can also be braided when it is wet and the braid left in all day. When evening comes and you undo the braids you will have a cascade of rippling, pre-Raphaelite curls.

If your hair does get tangled by the wind, untangle it gently by using a

Above: Slick short hair back with gel. Leave the gel in all day, then rinse out and style your hair in the evening. Photograph courtesy of Bain de Terre Spa Therapy.

BEFORE YOU GO

◯ Any hair coloring you are planning should be done at least one week prior to your holiday. This will allow the color to "soften" and allow time for some intensive conditioning on any dry ends.

◯ If you want to have a perm before your holiday, book the appointment at least three weeks before departure to allow your hair to settle. You will also have the opportunity to learn how best to manage your new style and help overcome any dryness.

◯ Remember to pack all your holiday hair needs – your favorite shampoos, conditioners, and styling products. And pack a selection of scarves and hair accessories. You will have more time to experiment on holiday.

◯ If possible take a travel dryer with dual voltage, and remember to pack an adaptor.

◯ Battery-powered stylers are convenient for holidays but remember to buy several replacements and to carry all the batteries separately from the styler. Airlines do not permit operational electric or battery powered accessories.

◯ Soft, bendy rollers are a good alternative to heated ones – they are also kinder to the hair.

◯ Have a trim before you go, but not a new style, as you won't want to worry about coping with a new look. Whatever you do, don't be tempted to have your hair cut abroad. Wait until you are back home and can visit your regular stylist.

Above: When the sun sets apply mousse to straightened hair and sleek back behind the ears, flicking the ends up. Then leave to dry naturally. By Jon Pereira-Santos, Montage Hair Company. Photography Suzy Corby.

Left: Breezy beach days whip the hair into a tangle. Take time to remove knots and snarls with a wide-toothed comb. Longer hair can be braided or knotted into a neat bun at the nape to keep it in place and prevent damage. Photograph courtesy of Silvikrin.

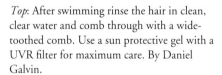

Top: After swimming rinse the hair in clean, clear water and comb through with a wide-toothed comb. Use a sun protective gel with a UVR filter for maximum care. By Daniel Galvin.

Above: To keep the hair in place, clasp it into a pretty barrette. Colorful accessories are great for the beach; take a selection to mix and match with your swimwear. By Daniel Galvin.

Opposite: To get separation on long curls mix a little conditioner with water and use a spray to mist the solution on to the hair. Scrunch the hair with your hands to create a casual look. Photograph courtesy of Bain de Terre Spa Therapy.

Opposite below: Pin fresh flowers in your hair for an alluring, feminine after-sun style. By Joseph and Jane Harling.

wide-toothed comb and work from the ends of the hair up towards the roots.

Keep your head and hair protected even when you are away from the beach. Wear a sun hat when shopping or sightseeing, especially at mid-day. When the sun sets, shampoo and condition your hair and, if possible, let it dry naturally. Leave heat styling for those special nights out.

WINTER HAIRCARE

During the winter, and particularly on a winter break, your hair will be exposed to damaging conditions, such as harsh biting winds and the drying effects of low temperatures and central heating. Central heating draws moisture from the hair and scalp, which causes static. Extreme cold makes the hair brittle and dry, and wet weather spells disaster for a style, making curly hair frizz and straight hair limp.

Above left: Long hair that is lightly layered gives lift on the crown and movement in the ends. For this look, rough-dry the hair and mist with styling lotion before setting on large rollers. When the hair is completely dry, lightly brush through to create soft waves and curls. By Taylor Ferguson.

Above: Short, naturally curly hair can be given a pretty style by drying it with a small round brush and working the hair upwards. By Andrew Collinge Photography Iain Philpott.

These effects can be counteracted with a few simple measures. To reduce the drying effects of central heating, place large bowls of water near the radiators or use humidifiers. Use a more intensive conditioner on your hair in the winter to combat dryness caused by cold. In damp weather apply a mousse, gel, or hairspray; they are invaluable for keeping a style in place and giving some degree of protection.

ON THE PISTE

❍ The sun's rays are intensified by reflection from the snow, so hair needs extra protection in the form of a hair sunscreen.
❍ Wind, blasts of snow, and sunshine are a damaging combination for hair, so wear a hat whenever possible.
❍ In freezing temperatures hair picks up static electricity, making it flyaway and unmanageable. Calm the static by spraying your brush with hairspray before brushing your hair.
❍ With sudden temperature changes – from icy cold slopes to a warm hotel – and constantly changing headgear your hair may need daily shampooing. Use a mild shampoo and light conditioner.

COLORING AND BLEACHING

Hair colorants have never been technically better; nowadays it is a simple matter to add a temporary tone and gloss to the hair or make a more permanent change. And there is a wide variety of home coloring products from which to choose.

THE CHOICE

Temporary colors are usually water-based and are applied to pre-shampooed, wet hair. They work by coating the outside, or cuticle layer, of the hair. The color washes away in the next shampoo. Temporary colors are good

---

FACT FILE

○ Coloring swells the hair shaft, making fine hair appear thicker.
○ Because color changes the porosity of the hair it can help combat oiliness.
○ Rich tones reflect more light and give hair a thicker appearance.
○ Highlights give fine hair extra texture and break up the heaviness of very thick hair.
○ Too light a hair color can make the hair appear thinner.

---

for a quick, but fleeting, change or for counteracting discoloration in blonde or white hair. Color-enhanced shampoos combine a color that washes out with a shampoo. They are similar to temporary colors, are easy to use, and are perfect for adding tone to gray, white, or bleached hair.

Semi-permanent colors give a more noticeable effect that lasts for six to eight shampoos. They can only add, enrich, or darken hair color, they cannot make it any lighter. Semi-permanent colors penetrate the cuticle and coat the outer edge of the cortex (the inner layer of the hair). The color fades gradually and is ideal for those who want to experiment but don't want to commit themselves to a more permanent change.

Longer lasting semi-permanent colors remain in the hair for 12-20 shampoos and are perfect for blending in the first gray hairs. The color penetrates even deeper into the cortex than in semi-permanent colors. This type is perfect for a more lasting change.

Permanent colors lighten or darken, and effectively cover white. The color enters the cortex during the development time (around 30 minutes) after which oxygen in the developer swells the pigments in the colorant, and holds them in. The roots may need retouching every six weeks. When retouching it is important to color only the new hair growth. If the new color overlaps previously treated hair there will be a build-up of color from the mid-lengths to the ends, which will make the hair more porous.

The model's fine hair was made to look thicker by working fine highlights of different tonal values throughout the hair. The feather cut was then styled forward and blow-dried into shape. A little wax was rubbed between the palms of the hands and applied to the hair with the fingertips to give further definition. By Nicky Clarke.

Below: Ash-blonde hair was tapered at the sides so that it feathered on to the face. Fine textured hair like this needs gentle styling to maintain it in good condition, especially after coloring, so regular conditioning treatments are essential. By Steven Carey.

Above: These copper tones were achieved by applying a permanent tint; the volume of hair was then increased by using a hot air brush to style the hair away from the face. You can get the same effect by working on one section of the hair at a time. Finish with firm-hold hairspray. Photograph courtesy of BaByliss.

Above: Here reddish hues were created with a longer-lasting semi-permanent color that added deep tones and luminosity. The hair was blow-dried straight, pointing the nozzle of the dryer downwards in order to polish and encourage the shine. By Yosh Toya, Photography Gen.

Above: Russet tones were further emphasized by weaving a few lighter colors into the front hair. The hair was blow-dried with styling gel to get lift at the roots. By Daniel Galvin.

Left: The model's hair was lightened to achieve this soft shade of blonde. Remember, only lift your hair color by one or two shades and don't forget that the roots will need retouching regularly. For this style the hair was graduated and blow-dried into shape. By Daniel Galvin.

A variety of herbs and other plants have been used in the past to color hair, and many of them have remained popular to this day. The natural dyes provide a semi-permanent color, although the results that can be achieved will vary. They depend on the quality of the raw ingredients combined with the natural color of the hair and how porous it is. Many top hairdressers mix their own vegetable dyes using a a wide range of ingredients, as well as using commercial colors. By Daniel Galvin.

NATURAL COLORING – HENNA

Vegetable colorants such as henna and camomile have been used since ancient times to color hair, and henna was particularly popular with the Ancient Egyptians. Although henna is the most widely used natural dye, others can be extracted from a wide variety of plants, including marigold petals, cloves, rhubarb stalks, and even tea leaves. Natural dyes work in much the same way as semi-permanent colorants by staining the outside of the hair. However, results are variable and a residue is often left behind, making further coloring with permanent tints or bleaches inadvisable.

Henna enhances natural highlights making color appear richer. It is available today as a powder, which is mixed with water to form a paste. The color fades gradually but frequent applications will give a stronger, longer-lasting effect. The result that is achieved when using henna depends on the natural color of the hair. On brunette or black hair it produces a lovely reddish glow, while lighter hair becomes a beautiful titian. Henna will not lighten, and it is not suitable for use on blonde hair. On hair that is more than 20 per cent gray, white, tinted, bleached, or highlighted, the resultant color will be orange.

The longer the henna is left on the hair, the more intense the result. Timings vary from one to two hours, but some Indian women leave henna on the hair for 24 hours, anointing their heads with oil to keep the paste supple.

The condition of the hair being treated is another factor that effects the intensity. The ends of long hair are always slightly lighter than the roots because they are more exposed to the sun, and henna will emphasize this effect. The resulting color will be darker on the roots to the mid-lengths and more vibrant from the mid-lengths to the ends.

It is always wise to test the henna you intend to use on a few loose hairs (the ones in your hairbrush will do),

noting the length of time it takes to produce the result you want.

Neutral henna can be used to add gloss and luster to the hair without adding any color. Mix the henna with water to a stiff paste. Stir in an egg yolk for extra conditioning, plus a little milk, which will help to keep the paste pliable. Apply to the hair and leave for an hour before rinsing thoroughly. Repeat every two to three months.

CAMOMILE

Camomile has a gentle lightening effect on hair and is good for sun-streaking blonde and light brown hair. However, it takes several applications and a good deal of time to produce the desired effect. The advantage of camomile over chemical bleach is that it never gives a brassy or yellow tone. Best for blonde hair, it will also gently lighten red.

To make a camomile rinse that can be used after each shampoo, add 2 tbsp

Above: Brunettes are very suitable candidates for having their hair colored. Their hair can be considerably enriched and enhanced with a henna, which will produce brilliant depths and tones. By Wella Living Colors.

Above right: These vibrant red tones were achieved using a mixture of vegetable dyes and by working highlights of different tones through the hair. The hair was then styled by blow-drying. By Daniel Galvin.

of dried camomile flowers to 1 pint of boiling water. Simmer for 15 minutes, strain and cool before use.

To obtain more positive results add 1 cup of dried camomile flowers to 1 cup of boiling water and leave to steep for 15 minutes. Cool, simmer, and strain. Stir in the juice of a fresh lemon along with 2 tbsp of a rich cream conditioner. Comb through the hair and leave to dry – in the sun, if possible. Finally, shampoo and condition your hair as usual.

DO'S AND DON'TS

❍ Do rinse henna paste thoroughly, or the hair and scalp will feel gritty.

❍ Don't expose hennaed hair to strong sunlight and always rinse salt and chlorine from the hair immediately after swimming.

❍ Do use a henna shampoo between color applications to enhance the tone.

❍ Don't use shampoos and conditioners containing henna on blonde hair, gray hair, or hair that has been chemically treated.

❍ Do use the same henna product each time you apply henna.

❍ Don't use compound henna (one that has had metallic salts added); it can cause long-term hair coloring problems.

CHOOSING A NEW COLOR

When choosing a color a basic rule is to keep to one or two shades at each side of your original tone. It is probably best to try a temporary colorant first; if you like the result you can choose a semi-permanent or permanent colorant next time. If you want to be a platinum blonde and you are a natural brunette, you should seek the advice of a professional hairdresser.

There are two important points to remember when considering a color change. First, only have a color change if your hair is in good condition; dry, porous hair absorbs color too rapidly, leading to a patchy result. Second, your make-up may need changing to suit your new color.

SPECIAL TECHNIQUES

Hairdressers have devised an array of coloring methods to create different effects. These include:

Hair painting, (flying colors) in which a combination of colors is applied with combs and brushes to the middle lengths and tips of the hair.

Highlights/lowlights, where fine strands of hair are tinted or bleached lighter or darker, or color is added just to give varying tones throughout the hair. This technique is sometimes called frosting or shimmering, particularly when bleach is used to give an overall lighter effect.

Slices, a technique in which assorted colors are applied through the hair to emphasize a cut and show movement.

COVERING WHITE HAIR

If you just want to cover a few white hairs use a temporary or semi-permanent color that will last for six to eight weeks. Choose one that is similar to your natural color. If the hair is brown, applying a warm brown color will pick out the white areas and give lighter chestnut highlights. Alternatively, henna will give a glossy finish, and at the same time produce stunning red highlights. For salt and pepper hair – hair with a

mixed amount of white with the natural color – try a longer lasting semi-permanent color. These last for up to 20 shampoos and also add shine.

When hair is completely white it can be covered with a permanent tint, but with this type of colorant it is necessary to update the color every four to six weeks, a fact that should be taken into consideration before choosing this option. Those who prefer to stay with their natural shade of white can improve on the color by using toning shampoos, conditioners, and styling products, which will remove any brassiness and add beautiful silvery tones.

CARING FOR COLORED HAIR

Chlorinated and salt water, perspiration, and the weather all conspire to fade colored hair, particularly red hair. However special products are available that will help counteract fading, such as those containing ultraviolet filters that protect colored hair from the effects of the sun. Other protective measures include rinsing the hair after swimming and using a shampoo designed for colored hair, followed by a separate conditioner. Gently blot the hair after shampooing – never rub it vigorously as this ruffles the cuticle and can result in color "escaping". Finally, use an intensive conditioning treatment at least once a month.

BLEACHING

Strictly speaking, anything that lightens the hair bleaches it, but in the present context bleaching refers specifically to any treatment that removes color from the hair – rather than adding color, which is the purpose of permanent colorants. There are several different types of bleach on the market and they range from the mild brighteners that lift hair color a couple of shades to the more powerful mixes that completely strip hair of its natural color.

Bleaching is quite difficult to do and is best left to a professional hair-

Left: There is a wide range of natural tones to choose from when you are looking for a new hair color.

Above: The alternative is to opt for more vibrant fashion shades. Color swatches courtesy of L'Oréal Coiffure.

dresser. If misused it can be very harsh and drying on the hair. To get the best results make sure your hair is in optimum condition prior to bleaching. Once the hair has been bleached, regular intensive conditioning treatments are essential.

COLOR CORRECTION

If you have been coloring your hair for some time and want to go back to your natural color and tone consult a professional hairdresser. Hair that has been tinted darker than its normal shade will have to be color-stripped with a bleach bath until the desired color is achieved. Hair that has been bleached or highlighted will need to be re-pigmented and then tinted to match the original color. For best results, all these processes must be carried out in a salon where the technicians have access to a variety of specialty products.

HELPFUL HINTS FOR HOME HAIR COLORING

Always read the directions supplied with the product before you start, and follow them precisely. Make sure you do a strand and skin sensitivity test, as detailed in the directions.

If you are retouching the roots of tinted or bleached hair, apply new color only to the regrowth area. Any overlap will result in uneven color and porosity, which in turn will adversely affect the condition of your hair.

Don't color your hair at home if the hair is split or visibly damaged, or if you have used bleach or any type of henna; you must allow previously treated hair to grow out before applying new color. Avoid coloring your hair if you are taking prescribed drugs, as the chemical balance of your hair can alter. Check with your family doctor first.

If your hair has been permed consult a hairdresser before using a hair colorant. And if you are in any doubt about using a color, always check with the manufacturer or consult a professional hair colorist.

FACT FILE

In the Middle Ages saffron and a mixture of sulfur, alum, and honey were used for bleaching and coloring hair. These concoctions were not always safe however, and in 1562 a certain Dr Marinello from Modena, Italy, wrote a treatise warning of the possible and undesirable consequences of bleaching the hair. He warned:
"The scalp could be seriously damaged and the hair be destroyed at the roots and fall out."

Top and above: Burnished Titian red tones give one of the most effective results when applied to natural brown hair. However reddish hues are particularly prone to fade so colored hair should be protected from the sun. Specialized shampoos and conditioners should be used to help maintain color. Photographs: top, Mark Hill for Wella; above, Zotos.

PERMANENT SOLUTIONS

Making straight hair curly is not a new idea. Women in Ancient Egypt coated their hair in mud, wound it around wooden rods and then used the heat from the sun to create the curls.

Waves that won't wash out are a more recent innovation. Modern perms were pioneered by A. F. Willat, who invented the "cold permanent wave" technique in 1934. Since then, improved formulations and ever more sophisticated techniques have made perms the most versatile styling option in hairdressing.

HOW THEY WORK

Perms work by breaking down inner structures (links) in your hair and re-forming them around a curler to give a new shape. Hair should be washed prior to perming as this causes the scales on the cuticles to rise gently, allowing the perming lotion to enter the hair shaft more quickly. The perming lotion alters the keratin and breaks down the sulfur bonds that link the fiber-like cells together in the inner layers of each hair. When these fibers have become loose, they can be formed into a new shape when the hair is stretched over a curler or a perming rod.

Once the curlers or rods are in place, more lotion is applied and the perm is left to develop to fix the new shape. The development time can vary according to the condition and texture of the hair. When the development is complete, the changed links in the hair are re-formed into their new shape by the application of a second chemical known as the neutralizer. The neutralizer contains an oxidizing agent that is effectively responsible for closing up the broken links and producing the wave or curl – permanently.

Specialist formulations enable your hairdresser to perm long hair while maintaining it in optimum condition. Here the hair was wound on to large rods to achieve a soft curl formation. Photograph courtesy of Clynol.

The type of curl that is produced depends on a number of factors. The size of the curler is perhaps the most important as this determines the size of the curl. Generally speaking the smaller the curler the smaller and therefore tighter the curl, whereas medium to large curlers tend to give a much looser effect. The strength of lotion used can also make a difference, as can the texture and type of hair. Hair in good condition takes a perm much better than hair in poor condition, and fine hair curls more easily than coarse hair.

After a perm it takes 48 hours for the keratin in the hair to harden naturally. During this time the hair is vulnerable to damage and must be treated with care. Resist shampooing, brushing, vigorous combing, blow-drying, or setting, any of which may cause the perm to drop.

Once hair has been permed it remains curly and shaped the way it has been formed, although new growth will be straight. As time goes by the curl can soften, and if the hair is long its weight may make the curl and the wave appear much looser.

HOME VERSUS SALON

Perming is such a delicate operation that many women prefer to leave it in the hands of experienced, professional hairdressers. The advantages of having hair permed in a salon are several. The hair is first analysed to see whether it is in fit condition to take a perm; colored, out-of-condition, or over-processed hair may not be suitable. With a professional perm there is also a greater choice in the type of curl – different strengths of lotion and different winding techniques all give a range of curls that are not available in home perms.

Above: Spiral perming gives a ringlet effect on long hair. It is important with hair of this length to re-perm only at the roots when the hair grows, or you may cause damage to previously permed hair. By Terence Renati.

POST PERM TIPS

❍ Don't wash newly permed hair for 48 hours after processing as any stress can cause curls to relax.
❍ Use shampoos and conditioners formulated for permed hair. They help retain the correct moisture balance and prolong the perm.
❍ Always use a wide-toothed comb and work from the ends upwards. Never brush the hair.
❍ Blot wet hair dry before styling to prevent stretching.
❍ Avoid using too much heat on permed hair. If possible, wash, condition, and leave to dry naturally.
❍ If your perm has lost its bounce, mist with water or try a curl reviver. These are designed to put instant volume and bounce into permed hair. They are also ideal for eliminating frizziness on naturally curly hair.
❍ Expect your perm to last three to six months, depending on the technique and lotion used.

Right: The model's thick hair was given a volume perm in order to produce a stunning style with the fullest look possible. By Kevin Murphy International for Clynol, Photography Martin Evening.

HOME RULES

If you do use a perm at home, it is essential that you read and follow the instructions supplied with the product. Remember to do a test curl to check whether your hair is suitable, and check to make certain you have enough curlers. You will probably want to enlist the help of a friend, as it's impossible to curl the back sections of your own hair properly, so you'll need a helping hand.

Timing is crucial – don't be tempted to remove the lotion before the time given or leave it on longer than directed.

Above: Short, straight hair was root permed and then blow-dried into place. By Paul Falltrick, Falltricks, for Clynol.

DON'T DO IT YOURSELF IF...

❍ Your hair is very dry or damaged.
❍ You have bleached or highlighted your hair: it may be too fragile. If in doubt, check with your hairdresser.
❍ The traces of an old perm still remain in your hair.
❍ You suffer from a scalp disorder such as eczema or have broken, irritated skin.

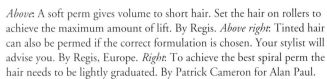

Above: A soft perm gives volume to short hair. Set the hair on rollers to achieve the maximum amount of lift. By Regis. *Above right:* Tinted hair can also be permed if the correct formulation is chosen. Your stylist will advise you. By Regis, Europe. *Right:* To achieve the best spiral perm the hair needs to be lightly graduated. By Patrick Cameron for Alan Paul.

SALON PERMS – THE CHOICES

Professional hairdressers can offer a number of different types of perm that are not available for home use:

Acid perms produce highly conditioned, flexible curls. They are ideally suited to hair that is fine, sensitive, fragile, damaged, or tinted, as they have a mildly acidic action that minimizes the risk of hair damage.

Alkaline perms give strong, firm curl results on normal and resistant hair.

Exothermic perms give bouncy, resilient curls. "Exothermic" refers to the gentle heat that is produced by the chemical reaction that occurs when the lotion is mixed. The heat allows the lotion to penetrate the hair cuticle, conditioning and strengthening the hair from inside as the lotion molds the hair into its new shape.

PERMING TECHNIQUES

Any of the above types of perm can be used with different techniques to produce a number of results.

Body perms are very soft, loose perms created by using large curlers, or sometimes rollers. The result is added volume with a hint of wave and movement rather than curls.

Root perms add lift and volume to the root area only. They give height and fullness, and are therefore ideal for short hair that tends to go flat.

Pin curl perms give soft, natural waves and curls, which are achieved by perming small sections of hair that have been pinned into pre-formed curls.

Stack perms give curl and volume to one-length hair cuts by means of different sized curlers. The hair on top of the head is left unpermed while the middle and ends have curl and movement.

Spiral perms create romantic spiral curls, an effect that is produced by winding the hair around special long curlers. The mass of curls makes long hair look much thicker.

Spot perms give support only on the area to which they are applied. For example, if the hair needs lift the perm is applied just on the crown. They can also be used on the fringe or side areas around the face.

Weave perms involve perming certain sections of hair and leaving the rest straight to give a mixture of texture and natural looking body and bounce, particularly on areas around the face such as the bangs.

REGROWTH PROBLEM

When a perm is growing out the areas of new growth can be permed if a barrier is created between old and new growth. The barrier can be a special cream or a plastic protector, both of which effectively prevent the perming lotion and neutralizer from touching previously permed areas.

There are also products that facilitate re-perming an entire length of hair without damaging the structure. These more complex solutions are only available from salons.

To keep a full perm looking its best, shampoo, apply mousse, then blow-dry using a diffuser or set the hair on rollers. By L'Oréal.

AFRICAN-AMERICAN HAIR

One of the most effective ways of styling very curly hair is to crop it close and short. With this type of cut you just need to shampoo, condition, and finish it with soft wax. By Macmillan.

African-American hair is fragile yet difficult to control, therefore it needs specialist care and pampering if it is to look its best.

This type of hair is almost always curly, although the degree of wave varies enormously. As a general rule, it is brittle and has a tendency to split and break. This is because the sebaceous glands produce insufficient sebum to moisturize the hair. In addition, because the hair is tightly curled, the sebum is unable to travel downwards to condition it naturally. If the curl forms kinks, this makes the hair thinner, and therefore weaker, at each bend.

Other types of black hair (e.g. Asian Amerian, Native American, Indians) can be very fine, making it difficult to style and set.

To treat excessive dryness choose a specialist formulation that replaces the natural oils lacking in black hair. If the product is massaged in daily, or whenever necessary, the hair will become more manageable with improved condition and shine. It is also important to deep condition the hair regularly.

STRAIGHTENING THE HAIR

Straightening, or relaxing, is in fact perming in reverse. A hair straightener, also known as a chemical relaxer, is combed or worked through the hair to change the structure and to straighten it. The result is permanent, only disappearing as the hair grows. Chemical relaxers come in different strengths to suit different hair textures and styles.

PROFESSIONAL TIP

Hair needs to be strong and healthy to take any type of chemical treatment. To check hair strength and natural elasticity, pluck out a hair and hold it firmly between the fingers of both hands, then pull gently. If the hair breaks with hardly any stretching, it is weak and in poor condition, in which case all chemical treatments should be avoided.

Before: Long, thick natural hair can be totally transformed with the technique known as weaving. To do this the hair is corn-row braided and then weaves are sewn on to the braided base.

After: Once the weave has been sewn into place, the new hair is cut and styled as desired. The result of all this work is a completely different look. By Eugene at Xtension Masters.

Hair that has been straightened is blow-dried using a vent brush. Straightening irons could also be used to achieve a similarly smooth effect. By Richard M F Mendleson of David's Hair Designers.

They are particularly effective on longer styles as the weight of the hair helps to maintain the straightened look. If you do this at home get advice first, and make sure you use high quality branded products and follow the instructions precisely to get the best results.

DEMI PERMING

Very curly hair can also be tamed by perming. This enables tight curls to be replaced by larger, looser ones. Demi-perms are good for short hair, giving a more controlled, manageable shape; on long hair they produce a softer, bouncier look. The more advanced perms involve softening the hair by weaving it on to rollers and then neutralizing it so that the curls are permanently set into their new shape.

To prevent frizziness and maintain the definition of curls, special lotions called curl activators and moisturizing sprays can be used to revive and preserve the formation of curls.

As with all chemical treatments, relaxing and perming can be potentially harmful to the hair, removing natural moisture and leaving hair in a weakened state. For this reason it is advisable to get skilled professional help and advice.

HOT COMBS

Before chemical relaxers became available the most popular hair straightening method was "hot pressing". This involved putting a pre-heated iron comb through the hair to loosen the curls. Up-to-date versions, called thermal texturizers, are electric pressing combs, which work in a similar way to loosen and soften very curly hair.

COLOR OPTIONS

Because of its natural dryness and porosity, black hair should be colored with caution, preferably by a professional hairdresser. If the hair has been straightened, relaxed, or permed it may be too weak to color successfully.

Techniques such as highlighting, low-lighting, or tipping the ends are best for this type of hair.

SPECIAL PROBLEMS

Traction hair loss is caused by braiding or weaving hair too tightly. If the hair is pulled too forcibly too often, it will disrupt the hair follicles, cause scar tissue to form and, ultimately, hair loss. To help prevent this, avoid braiding or pulling the hair into tight braids. Similar problems can also result from misusing perming and relaxing chemicals.

KEEPING BLACK HAIR BEAUTIFUL

○ Use a wide-toothed afro comb for curly hair and a natural bristle brush for relaxed hair. Combing will help spread the natural oils through the hair, making it look shinier and healthier. Use intensive pre-shampoo treatments.

○ Massage the scalp regularly to encourage oil production.

○ Shampoo as often as you feel necessary but only lather once, using a small amount of shampoo. Rinse thoroughly. Towel-blot, don't rub hair.

○ Once a month try a hot oil treatment, which will lubricate dry scalp conditions as well as moisturize brittle hair.

○ If you have delicate bangs or baby fine hair around the hairline (sometimes from breakage, sometimes an inherited trait), use a tiny round brush and a hairdryer to blend in this hair.

○ Gels are good for molding black hair into shape; choose non-oily formulas that give hair a healthy sheen.

○ If you use hot combs or curling tongs, make sure you shield the hair by using a protective product.

○ For extra hold and added shine use a finishing spray.

○ Braided hair needs a softening shampoo that maintains the moisture balance and helps eliminate a dry scalp.

After straightening or relaxing, Afro-American hair can be styled smooth using blow-drying techniques. *Left*: The hair has been smoothed into curls. *Center*: Here it has been flicked up at the ends and the bangs curved. *Right*: For this style it was piled into soft curls and given fuller bangs. By Richard M F Mendleson, David's Hair Designers.

SUCCESSFUL STYLING

Successful styling means choosing a hairstyle that suits your looks and lifestyle, and then learning the techniques that will ensure a perfect finish. Today there is an enormous range of gadgets, hair products, and heated styling equipment available to the general public, all of which, used properly, can effect wonderful transformations. The trick is to know what to use and when to use it in order to achieve the desired results. Here we show you how.

CHOOSING A STYLE TO SUIT YOUR FACE

Make the most of your looks by choosing a style that maximizes your best features. The first feature you should consider is your face shape – is it round, oval, square, or long? If you are not sure what shape it is then the easiest way to find out is to scrape your hair back off your face. Stand squarely in front of a mirror and use a lipstick to trace the outline of your face on to the mirror. When you stand back you should be able to see into which of the following categories your face shape falls.

THE SQUARE FACE

The square face is angular with a broad forehead and a square jawline. To make the best of this shape, choose a hairstyle with long layers, preferably one with soft waves or curls, as these create a softness that detracts from the hard lines. The hair should be parted at the side of the head and any bangs combed away from the face.
Styles to avoid: Severe geometric cuts – they will only emphasize squareness; long bobs with heavy bangs; severe styles in which the hair is scraped off the face and parted down the center.

THE ROUND FACE

On the round face the distance between the forehead and the chin is about equal to the distance between the cheeks. Choose a style with short bangs, which lengthens the face, and a short cut, which makes the face look thinner.
Styles to avoid: Curly styles, because they emphasize the roundness; very full, long hair or styles that are scraped right back off the face.

THE OVAL FACE

The oval face has wide cheekbones that taper down into a small, often pointed, chin, and up to a fairly narrow forehead. This is regarded by many experts as the perfect face shape. If your face is oval in shape then you have the advantage of being able to wear any hairstyle you choose.

THE LONG FACE

The long face is characterized by a high forehead and long chin, and needs to be given the illusion of width. Soften the effect with short layers, or go for a bob with bangs, which will create horizontal lines. Scrunch-dried or curly bobs balance a long face.
Styles to avoid: Styles without bangs, and long, straight, blunt cuts.

THE COMPLETE YOU

When choosing a new style you should also take into account your overall body shape. If you are a traditional pear-shape don't go for elfin styles; they will draw attention to the lower half of your body, making your hips look even wider. Petite women should avoid masses of very curly hair as this makes the head appear larger and out of proportion with the body.

IF YOU WEAR GLASSES . . .

Try to choose frames and a hairstyle that complement each other. Large spectacles could spoil a neat, feathery cut, and very fine frames could be overpowered by a large, voluminous style. Remember to take your glasses to the salon when having your hair restyled, so that your stylist can take their shape into consideration when deciding on the overall effect.

SPECIFIC PROBLEMS

○ Prominent nose: incorporate softness into your style.
○ Pointed chin: style hair with width at the jawline.
○ Low forehead: choose a style with wispy bangs, rather than one with full bangs.
○ High forehead: disguise with bangs.
○ Receding chin: select a style that comes just below chin level, with waves or curls.
○ Uneven hairline: bangs should conceal this problem.

Left: Wispy bangs stylishly disguise a low forehead. Hair by Sam Mcknight for Silvikrin. *Above*: A high forehead or uneven hairline can be hidden under full bangs. Hair by Paul Falltrick, Photography Iain Philpott. *Below*: Strong features benefit from a soft, full hairstyle. Hair by Jed Hamill of Graham Webb International for Clynol, Photography Ian Hooton.

STYLE GALLERY, SHORT HAIR

Short hair can be cut close,
cropped, or layered in a variety
of styles.

Fine, straight hair was lightly layered and
cut close into the nape. A root perm
provided extra volume at the crown of the
head. The hair was then finger-dried using
a styling mousse. By Yosh Toya,
Photography Gen.

Naturally wavy hair was lightly layered to
encourage movement. A wet-look gel was
applied and the hair was combed into soft
waves and side curls, then left to dry
naturally. By Regis, Photography John
Swannell.

Naturally wavy hair was cut into a one-
length bob and taken behind the ears,
using wet-look gel to give definition and
accentuate the waves. By Regis,
Photography John Swannell.

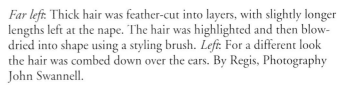

Far left: Thick hair was feather-cut into layers, with slightly longer lengths left at the nape. The hair was highlighted and then blow-dried into shape using a styling brush. *Left*: For a different look the hair was combed down over the ears. By Regis, Photography John Swannell.

Left: Fine hair was softly layered and given an application of mousse, then the hair was ruffle-dried with the fingers to create just a little lift at the roots. *Right*: The same haircut was blow-dried forwards using a styling brush. By Regis, Photography John Swannell.

Medium-textured hair was cut into face-framing layers. Mousse was applied from the roots to the ends, then the hair was blow-dried forwards, using the fingers to rake through the hair from the back to the front. By Paul Falltrick, Falltricks, for Clynol, Photography Alistair Hughes.

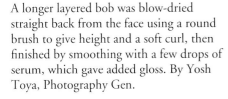

A longer layered bob was blow-dried straight back from the face using a round brush to give height and a soft curl, then finished by smoothing with a few drops of serum, which gave added gloss. By Yosh Toya, Photography Gen.

Medium-textured hair was cut into layers of the same length, then blow-dried using a strong-hold mousse to get lift, and finished with a mist of firm-hold hairspray. By Daniel Galvin.

A short, urchin cut is good for all hair textures. Highlights give extra interest and add thickness to finer hair. By Nicky Clarke, Photography Paul Cox.

A short, feathery cut was set off with straight, cropped bangs. For this style the hair can either be left to dry naturally, or blow-dried while ruffling with the fingers. By Anestis Kyprianou of Cobella for Schwarzkopf, Photography Martin Evening.

Medium-textured hair was graduated to give this head-hugging cut. Mousse was applied from the roots to the ends, then the hair was blow-dried forwards from the crown. By Neville Daniel for Lamaur.

Very curly, wiry hair was cropped close to the head, then dressed using just a little wax to give definition and separation. By Frank Hession, for L'Oréal Coiffure.

This soft style is ideal for hair with more than a hint of natural wave; layering gives additional movement. After an application of a little mousse (styling gel would be equally suitable) the hair was left to dry naturally, occasionally running the fingers through to encourage curl. By Beverly Kyprianou of Cobella for Schwarzkopf, Photography Martin Evening.

Thick hair was razor cut to give forward movement, then blow-dried for a few seconds with the dryer set on high heat, at the same time brushing in all directions to give extra movement. By John Frieda.

A short cut was given extra interest by bleaching the hair honey-blonde. It was then blow-dried into shape and finished using wax to create separation. By Yosh Toya, Photography Gen.

One-length hair was parted at the side and slicked down with a wet-look gel to create this slick style. Pictures left to right by Joseph and Jane Harling, Photography Ruth Crafer.

Fine hair was softly layered and combed forwards. A little wax was rubbed between the palms and applied with the fingertips to strands of hair in order to achieve separation.

A thick, one-length bob was blow-dried very smooth from a side parting. The hair was misted with hairspray and smoothed with the hands to eliminate wisps.

Wispy, fine hair was given extra volume with a light perm, then blow-dried forwards. A semi-permanent color gives this type of hair added depth.

Choppy layers give an uneven texture to this thick hair. The hair was blow-dried using mousse and a styling brush to create lift. By Alan Edwards for L'Oréal Coiffure.

A root perm helped to give lift at the crown on this short, layered look. Mousse was applied to give extra lift and the hair was blow-dried forwards from the crown. By Neville Daniel, Photography Will White.

Very straight hair was cut into a neat, face-framing shape, then blow-dried forwards. It was then finished with a mist of shine spray for added gloss. By Andrew Collinge and Harrods, Photography Iain Philpott.

STYLE GALLERY, MID-LENGTH HAIR

Hair of medium length can be worn in a sleek bob or lightly layered to give versatility.

Layering gives this 70s inspired style a fresh look. The hair was misted with styling spray and rough-dried before finishing with a little gloss. By Trevor Sorbie, Photography Mark Havrilliak.

Above: Fine mid-length hair can be made to look thicker by blunt cutting just below ear level. This style can be roller-set and brushed through with a bristle brush to smooth, or simply blow-dried with a round brush. For L'Oréal.

Medium-textured hair was cut into a one-length bob. Styling spray was applied to partially dried hair, which was then wound on large rollers and heat set. After the rollers were removed the hair was brushed into shape. By Charles Worthington, Worthingtons, for L'Oréal Coiffure.

A longer, one-length, graduated bob is perfect for thick, straight hair. Add extra shine by using a longer-lasting semi-permanent color. By Umberto Giannino, for L'Oréal Coiffure.

A mid-length bleached bob was scrunch-dried with mousse to give a tousled look. Use a diffuser to encourage more volume. By Stuart Kirby of Eaton Hair Group for L'Oréal Coiffure.

A layered cut was permed to give lots of movement. The hair was scrunch-dried, with the head held forward to give maximum volume. By Anthony Mascolo, Toni & Guy for L'Oréal Coiffure.

A bob was highlighted using a light, golden-blonde color to give natural, warm lights, then styled and blow-dried using a soft sculpting spray. By Barbara Daley Hair Studio, for L'Oréal Coiffure.

A razor-cut bob gives graduation so the hair moves freely. The hair was colored with a shade of mahogany to give more depth, and then blow-dried using mousse. For L'Oréal.

Left: Thick hair was cut into a bob, then sprayed with styling lotion before setting on large rollers. After drying, the hair was brushed through to give a smooth style that is full of volume. *Right:* The same cut was blow-dried smooth using a styling brush. By Mod Hair, for Schwarzkopf.

A smooth, graduated bob was cut long at the sides and shorter into the back. To add additional tone and shine use a longer-lasting semi-permanent color, which also gives gloss. Blow-dry straight using a styling brush to smooth the ends under. For L'Oréal.

Left: Natural movement was encouraged by blunt cutting and leaving the hair to dry naturally. Alternatively, the hair could be dried using a flat diffuser attachment on the dryer. *Right*: The same style was sprayed with styling lotion and set on large rollers. When the rollers were removed the hair was ruffled through with the fingers, not brushed. By Regis, Photography John Swannell.

Thick, straight hair was heavily highlighted and cut into a blunt, short bob. Either blow-dry or leave to dry naturally. By Yosh Toya, Photography Gen.

Left: Wavy hair was cut in short layers. Layers encourage more curl and movement and give a soft, feminine style. The hair was dried using mousse and lifted with the fingers while drying to get height on the crown. By Cobella, for Schwarzkopf, Photography Martin Evening.

Left: A soft body perm gives volume to this one-length bob. The hair was gently dried using mousse for additional lift. By Yosh Toya, Photography Gen.

STYLE GALLERY, LONG HAIR

Long hair can be waved,
curled, or left to fall free.

Naturally wavy hair was roller-set and heat-dried before brushing through lightly. A similar look could be achieved with a soft perm. By Steven Carey.

After an application of styling spray the hair was set on large rollers. When dry the hair was combed to one side and allowed to fall into soft waves, with a tiny tendril pulled in front of one ear. By Neville Daniel, for Lamur.

Above. Long, straight hair was graduated at the sides to give interest. It was then shampooed and conditioned, and left to dry naturally. By Neville Daniel, for Lamaur.

A vegetable color adds depth and makes hair appear even thicker. The hair was then simply styled by blow-drying. By Daniel Galvin.

Soft, undulating waves were achieved by tonging the hair, then lightly combing it through. Spray shine was applied to the finish. By Nicky Clarke.

Thick hair was cut with graduated sides and a heavy fringe to give this 60s look. The hair can be blow-dried smooth or left to dry naturally. By John Frieda.

Setting lotion was applied to clean hair, which was set on large rollers and heat dried. When the hair was completely dry the rollers were removed and the hair gently back combed at the roots to give even more height and fullness. By Daniel Galvin.

Far left: The hair was shampooed and conditioned, then rough-dried before applying mousse and setting on heated rollers. The hair was then brushed through into soft waves. *Left*: This alternative style was achieved by tonging. It could also be set on shapers. For Silvikrin.

Left: A thick graduated cut was given maximum lift by spraying the roots with gel spray and backcombing lightly, then brushing over the top layers. By Daniel Galvin.

Naturally wavy hair was lightly layered, then set on large rollers. When the hair was dry it was brushed lightly to give broken up waves and curls. By Daniel Galvin.

The hair was sprayed with styling lotion and set on heated rollers. When it was dry a bristle brush was used to smooth it into waves. By Adam Lyons, for L'Oréal Coiffure.

Above: Coarse hair was rough-dried and then tonged all over before brushing through to give a soft movement. By Keith Harris for Braun.

Left: Long, straight hair was blunt-cut at the ends and simply styled from a center parting. By Taylor Ferguson.

Left: To give one-length hair extra body the head was tipped forwards and the hair misted with sculpting lotion. The roots were scrunched a little with the hands before straightening the head. By Paul Falltrick, Falltricks, for Clynol, Photography Alistair Hughes.

TAKE ONE GIRL
The following styles illustrate how one-length hair can be transformed using different styling techniques.

1 Soft waves were created with rollers.

2 The top hair was clipped up and the back hair tonged into tendrils.

3 High bunches were carefully secured and the hair crimped.

4 The top hair was secured on the crown. A band was wrapped with a small piece of hair and the length allowed to fall freely.

5 The hair was clipped back and two simple braids were worked at each side.

Hair by Taylor Ferguson.

STYLE GALLERY, SPECIAL OCCASIONS

These styles will inspire you when you want to dress up long hair on those special occasions.

The hair was softly scooped into large curls and pinned in place. One tendril was left to fall free to soften the style. By Zotos International.

The hair was secured in a very high ponytail on the crown, then divided into sections and looped into curls. If your hair isn't long enough for this style, you could use a hairpiece. By Steven Carey, Photography Alistair Hughes.

Vibrant blond and copper lights add brilliance to the hair. The front hair was sectioned off and the back hair secured in a high ponytail. The hair was then divided and coiled into loops before pinning in place. The front hair was smoothed over and secured at the back. For Schwarzkopf.

The foundation for this style came from a roller-set. The back hair was then formed into a French pleat and the top hair looped, curled and pinned into place. The side tendrils were allowed to fall free. Hair by Regis, Photography Mark York.

Very curly hair was simply twisted up at the back and secured with pins. Curls were allowed to fall down on one side to give a feminine look. By Steven Carey, Photography Alistair Hughes.

Long hair was scooped up, but the essence of this style is to allow lots of strands to fall in soft curls around the face. By Partners.

A high ponytail forms the basis of this style. The hair was then looped into curls and pinned, and the bangs were combed to one side. Hair by Keith Harris for Braun.

THE SALON VISIT

London hairdresser Nicky Clarke always explains to his clients how to style their hair at home.

A professional cut is the basis of any style. Expert stylists evaluate your hair and lifestyle before they even pick up a pair of scissors. The best way to choose a salon is by personal recommendation. If a friend has a good haircut ask them for the name of their hairdresser. If this is not possible you will have to do some research.

See if there are any salons in your area that look promising. Remember that the exterior can be deceptive, so have a look at the interior as well. The salon should be clean and welcoming, with a style and ambience that appeals to you, and sales material that is new and fresh. The stylists should also reflect an image that you like.

THE FIRST VISIT

Once you have chosen a salon, make an appointment for a consultation. Wear clothes that reflect your lifestyle; for example, if you are a bank teller, don't wear a track-suit – you will give the stylist the wrong impression. Discuss your hair's idiosyncrasies and explain what you like and dislike about it. Spare a few minutes to discuss how you are going to manage the style between salon visits. If you want a wash-and-wear style that falls into place with the flick of a comb, say so. If you are prepared to spend 15 minutes a day scrunching a perm to perfection, then speak up.

Hairdressers are not mind readers: neither can they wave a magic wand. However they can, with technical expertise, make the most of any type of hair. Listen to what they offer, but never be coerced into something with which you don't feel happy. Good hairdressers translate fashion trends into what is right for you. Yet you must be realistic; if your hair is thick and curly it will never hang in a straight, shiny bob, no matter how good the cut.

TAKING NOTES

While you are having your hair done, watch how your stylist does your hair, how much mousse or gel they apply and how they dry your hair. A good haircut should need the minimum of styling products and drying to achieve the desired result. Ask for advice on how to achieve the same look at home.

As a general rule, you need to have your hair cut every six to eight weeks, and to have a tint or color regrowth every four weeks; a highlight root application needs to be done at least every three months, and perms every four to six months.

TECHNICAL SKILL

With such a wide variety of perms and colors available in drug stores you may wonder why you should visit a salon to have your hair colored or permed. Yet the fact is that what you are buying is expertise and artistry. At the salon the stylist will use techniques that can be varied to suit the individual's specific hair textures and solve specific problems. For example, colors can be blended and applied in various ways to achieve a wide range of effects; hair can be made to look thicker and glossier by color shading; perms can be used to give body, not just curl; long hair can be spiral or corkscrew-permed for movement; and special products can be used to refresh colors and reactivate curls.

COMPLAINTS

If you are not satisfied with the service you have received, then complain. Ask to see the salon manager, explain the problem, and ask what they are prepared to do about it. You should expect an apology, but don't expect to be offered a refund. If your hair has been badly permed, don't accept any offer to have it re-permed. The remedy is to have a course of intensive conditioning treatments. Following this you should wait until the hair is in optimum condition before you have another perm or colour. If it is just a question of not liking the style, then that is a matter for discussion.

If you suffer serious damage, for example, an itchy burning scalp, blisters, cuts, hair breakage, or hair loss, then immediately seek advice from your family doctor or a trichologist. In the majority of cases remedial treatment should be prescribed and the damage minimized. If the practitioner feels that you have cause for complaint and compensation, then the practitioner should prepare a report giving full details and an analysis of the problem. However, remember that hair grows, blisters heal, and memories fade. So, act quickly and,

if necessary, make certain you have some photographs taken to reinforce your claim.

IMAGING

Imaging, which is available in some salons, is a means of previewing yourself on a video screen wearing a range of haircuts and colors. It is invaluable for experimenting with different looks before making a commitment to a particular style. Developed in France, the system is designed to take the stress out of choosing a style.

Watch how your stylist dries your hair. Here Trevor Sorbie, lifts the front hair to create lift and movement.

STYLING TOOLS

The right tools not only make hair-styling more fun, but also makes it much easier. Brushes, combs, and pins are the basic tools of styling. The following is a guide to help you choose what is most suitable from the wide range that is available.

BRUSHES

Brushes are made of bristles (sometimes termed quills or pins), which may be natural hog bristle, plastic, nylon, or wire. The bristles are embedded in a wooden, plastic, or molded rubber base and set in tufts or rows. This allows loose or shed hair to collect in the grooves without interfering with the action of the bristles. The spacing of the tufts plays an important role – generally, the wider the spacing between the rows of bristles the easier the brush will flow through the hair.

The role of brushing

Brushes help to remove tangles and knots and generally smooth the hair. The action of brushing from the roots to the ends removes dead skin cells and dirt, and encourages the cuticles to lie flat, thus reflecting the light. Brushing also stimulates the blood supply to the hair follicles, promoting healthy growth.

Natural bristles

Natural bristles are made of natural keratin (the same material as hair) and therefore create less friction and wear on the hair. They are good for grooming and polishing, and help to combat static on flyaway hair. However, they will not penetrate wet or thick hair and you must use a softer bristle brush for fine or thinning hair. In addition, the sharp ends can scratch the scalp.

Plastic, nylon, or wire bristles

All of these bristles are easily cleaned and heat resistant, so they are good for blow-drying. They are available in a variety of shapes and styles. Cushioned brushes give good flexibility, as they glide through the hair, preventing tugging and helping to remove knots. They are also non-static.

A major disadvantage is that the ends can be harsh, so try to choose bristles with rounded or ball tips.

TYPES OF BRUSH

Circular or radial brushes come in a variety of sizes and are circular or semi-circular in shape. These brushes have either mixed bristles for finishing, a rubber pad with nylon bristles, or metal pins for styling. They are used to tame and control naturally curly, permed, and wavy hair and are ideal for blow-drying. The diameter of the brush determines the resulting volume and movement, much the same way as rollers do.

Flat or half-round brushes are ideal for all aspects of wet or dry hairstyling and blow-drying. Normally they are made of nylon bristles in a rubber base. Some bases slide into position on to the plastic molded handle. Rubber bases can be removed for cleaning and replacement bristles are sometimes available.

Pneumatic brushes have a domed rubber base with bristles set in tufts. They can be plastic, natural bristle, or both.

Vent brushes have vented hollow centers that allow the air flow from the dryer to pass through them. Special bristle, or pin, patterns are designed to lift and disentangle even wet hair. Vents and tunnel brush heads enable the air to circulate freely through both the brush and the hair so the hair dries faster.

COMBS

Choose good quality combs with saw-cut teeth. This means that each individual tooth is cut into the comb, so there are no sharp edges. Avoid cheap plastic combs that are made in a mold and so form lines down the center of every tooth. They are sharp, and gradually scrape away the cuticles layers of the hair, causing damage and often breakage.

Use a wide-toothed comb for disentangling and combing conditioner through the hair. Fine tail-combs are for styling; Afro combs for curly hair; and styling combs for grooming.

PINS AND CLIPS

These are indispensable for sectioning and securing hair during setting, and for putting hair up. Most pins are available with untipped, plain ends, or cushion tipped ends. Non-reflective finishes are available, so the pins are less noticeable in the hair, and most are made of metal, plastic, or stainless steel. Colors include brown, black, gray, blonde, white, and silver.

Double-pronged clips are most frequently used for making pin or barrel curls. Grips give security to curls, French pleats, and all upswept styles. In North America they are known as "Bobby" pins, in Britain as "Blendrites" and "Kirbis". To avoid discomfort, position grips in the hair so that the flat edge rests towards the scalp.

Heavy hairpins are made of strong metal and come either waved or straight. They are ideal for securing rollers and when putting hair up.

Fine hairpins are used for dressing hair. They are quite delicate and prone to bend out of shape, so they should only be used to secure small amounts of hair. These pins are easily concealed, especially if you use a matching color. They are sometimes used to secure pin curls during setting, rather than using heavier clips, which can leave a mark.

Sectioning clips are clips with a single prong, and are longer in length than other clips. They are most often used for holding hair while working on another section, or securing pin curls.

Twisted pins are fashioned like a screw and are used to secure chignons and French pleats.

ROLLERS

Rollers vary in diameter, length, and the material from which they are made.

Smooth rollers, that is, those without spikes or brushes, will give the sleekest finish, but are more difficult to put in. More popular are brush rollers, especially the self-fixing variety that do not need pins or clips.

SOFT ROLLERS

Soft rollers were inspired by the principle of rag-rolling hair. Soft 'twist tie' rollers are made from pliable rubber, plastic, or cotton fabric and provide one of the more natural ways to curl hair. In the center of each roller is a tempered wire, which enables it to be bent into shape. The waves or curls that are produced are soft and bouncy and the technique is gentle enough for permed or tinted hair.

To use, section clean, dry hair and pull to a firm tension, 'trapping' the end in a roller that you have previously doubled over. Roll down to the roots of the hair and fold over to secure. Leave in for 30-60 minutes without heat, or for 10-15 minutes if you apply heat. If you twist the hair before curling you will achieve a more voluminous style.

STYLE EASY

The combination of practice and the right styling product enables you to achieve a salon finish at home. The products listed below enable you to do it in style.

GELS

Gels come in varying degrees of viscosity, from a thick jelly to a liquid spray. They are sometimes called sculpting lotions and are used for precise styling. Use them to lift roots, tame wisps, create tendrils, calm static, heat set, and give structure to curls. Wet gel can be used for sculpting styles.

TIP
A gel can be revitalized the following day by running wet fingers through the hair, against the direction of the finished look.

HAIRSPRAY

Traditionally, hairspray was used to hold a style in place; today varying degrees of stiffness are available to suit all needs. Use hairspray to keep the hair in place, get curl definition when scrunching, and mist over rollers when setting.

Hairsprays are available in a variety of formulations, including light and firm holds. Photography by Silvikrin

TIPS
○ A light application of spray on a hair brush can be used to tame flyaway ends.
○ Use hairspray at the roots and tong or blow-dry the area to get immediate lift.

MOUSSE

Mousse is the most versatile styling product. It comes as a foam and can be used on wet or dry hair. Mousses contain conditioning agents and proteins to nurture and protect the hair. They are available in different strengths, designed to give soft to maximum holding power, and can be used to lift flat roots or smooth frizz. Use when blow-drying, scrunching, and diffuser drying.

TIPS
○ Make sure you apply mousse from the roots to the ends, not just in a blob on the crown.
○ Choose the right type for your hair. Normal is good for a great many styles, but if you want more holding power, don't just use more mousse as it can make hair dull; instead, choose a firm or maximum-hold product.

SERUMS

Serums, glossers, polishes, and shine sprays are made from oils or silicones, which improve shine and softness by forming a microscopic film on the surface of the hair. Formulations can vary from light and silky to heavier ones with a distinct oily feel. They also contain substances designed to smooth the cuticle, encouraging the tiny scales to lie flat and thus reflect the light and make the hair appear shiny. Use these products to improve the feel of the hair, to combat static, de-frizz, add shine and gloss, and temporarily repair split ends.

TIP
Don't use too much serum or you will make your hair oily.

STYLING OR SETTING LOTIONS

Styling lotions contain flexible resins that form a film on the hair and aid setting, and protect the hair from heat damage. There are formulations for dry, colored or sensitized hair; others give volume and additional shine. Use for roller-setting, scrunching, blow-drying, and natural drying.

TIP
If using a styling lotion for heat setting look out for formulations that offer thermal protection.

WAXES, POMADES, AND CREAMS

These products are made from natural waxes, such as carnauba (produced by a Brazilian palm tree), which are softened with other ingredients such as mineral oils and lanolin to make them pliable. Both soft and hard formulations are available. Some pomades contain vegetable wax and oil to give gloss and sheen. Other formulations produce foam and are water soluble, and leave no residue. Use for dressing the hair and for controlling frizz and static.

When applying mousse use a "handful", and make sure you distribute it evenly. By Clynol.

APPLIANCES

Heated styling appliances allow you to style your hair quickly, efficiently, and easily. A wide range of heated appliances is available.

AIR WAVERS

Air wavers combine the efficiency of a blow-dryer with the convenience of a styling wand. They operate on the same principle as a blow-dryer, blowing warm air though the shaft. Many wavers are available with a variety of clip-on options, including brushes, prongs, and tongs, some with retractable teeth. Use for creating soft waves and volume at the roots.

> **TIP**
> Apply a styling spray or lotion before air waving and style the hair while it is still damp.

CRIMPERS

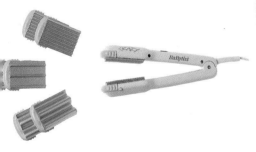

Crimpers consist of two ridged metal plates that produce uniform patterned crimps in straight lines in the hair. The hair must be straightened first, either by blow-drying or using flat irons. The crimper is then used to give waves or ripples. Some crimpers have reversible or dual-effect styling plates to give different effects. Use for special styling effects or to increase volume.

> **TIPS**
> ○ Do not use on damaged, bleached, or over-stressed hair.
> ○ Brushing crimped hair gives a softer result.

BLOW-DRYERS

Choose a dryer that has a range of heat, speed settings so that the hair can be power-dried on high heat, finished on a lower heat, and then used with cool air to set the style. The life expectancy of a blow-dryer averages between 200-300 hours. Use for blow-drying.

> **TIPS**
> ○ Always point the airflow down the hair shaft to smooth the cuticle and encourage shine.
> ○ Take care not to hold the dryer too near the scalp; it can cause burns.
> ○ When you have finished blow-drying allow the hair to cool thoroughly, then check that the hair is completely dry. Warm hair often gives the illusion of dryness while it is, in fact, still damp.
> ○ Never use a dryer without its filter in place – hair can easily be drawn into the machine.

The blow-dryer is an essential piece of equipment, particularly when you need to dry your hair in a hurry. Photograph courtesy of BaByliss.

DIFFUSERS AND NOZZLES

Originally, diffusers were intended for drying curly hair slowly, in this way encouraging curl formation for scrunched styles. The diffuser serves to spread the airflow over the hair so the curls are not literally blown away. The prongs on the diffuser head also help to increase volume at the root and give lift. Diffusers with flat heads are designed for gentle drying without ruffling, and are more suitable for shorter styles. The newest type of diffuser has long, straight prongs which are designed to inject volume into straight hair while giving a smooth finish. Nozzles fit over the end of the barrel of the blow-dryer and are used to give precise direction when styling.

HEATED ROLLERS

HOT BRUSHES

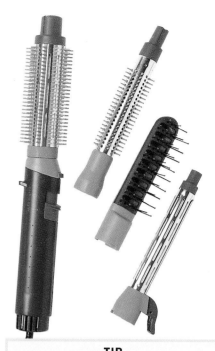

Heated rollers are available in sets and normally comprise a selection of around 20 small, medium, and large rollers, with color-coded clips to match. The early models came with spikes, which many women prefer because they have a good grip. New developments include ribbed rubber surfaces, which are designed to be kinder to the hair; curved barrel shapes that follow the form of the head, and clip fasteners are more recent innovations

The speed at which the rollers heat up varies, depending on the type of roller. PTC (positive temperature co-efficient) element rollers heat up fastest because they have an element inside each roller, and the heat is transferred directly from the base to the roller. Wax-filled rollers take longer, around 15 minutes, but they retain their temperature over a longer period. All rollers cool down completely in 30 minutes. Use heated rollers for quick sets, to give curl and body. They are ideal for preparing long hair for dressing.

Hot brushes are easier to handle than tongs, and come in varying sizes for creating curls of different sizes. Wind down the length of the hair, hold for a few seconds until the heat has penetrated through the hair, then gently remove. Cordless hot brushes, which use batteries to produce heat, are also available and are very convenient for travel. Use for root lift, curl, and movement.

When using a hot brush make certain you follow the manufacturer's instructions carefully. Photograph courtesy BaByliss.

STRAIGHTENERS

Straighteners, or flat irons, are based on the same principle as crimpers but have flat plates to iron out frizz or curl. Use for "pressing" really curly hair.

TIPS

○ Use a styling spray before heat straightening.
○ Straighteners are designed for occasional, not daily, use, as they work at a high temperature, which can cause damage to the hair.

TONGS

Tongs consist of a barrel, or prong, and a depressor groove. The barrel is round: the depressor is curved to fit around the barrel when the tong is closed. The thickness of the barrel varies, and the size of the tong that is used depends on whether small, medium, or large curls are required.

TIPS

○ Be careful when tonging white or bleached hair as it can discolor.
○ Always use tongs on dry, not wet, hair.
○ If curling right up to the roots, place a comb between the tongs and the scalp so the comb forms a barrier against the heat.
○ Leave tonged curls to cool before styling.

TRAVEL DRYERS

Travel dryers are ideal for taking on vacation. They are usually miniature versions of standard dryers, and some are even available with their own small diffusers. Check that the dryer you buy has dual voltage and a travel case.

Keep vacation haircare to a minimum by making use of dual-purpose heated appliances. Don't forget to pack a universal plug when travelling to other countries. Photograph courtesy of Silvikrin.

SAFETY TIPS

○ Equipment should be unplugged when not in use.
○ Never use electric equipment with wet hands, and don't use near water.
○ Only use one appliance for each socket outlet – adaptors may cause overload.
○ The cord should not be wrapped tightly around the equipment; coil it loosely before storing.
○ Tongs can be cleaned by wiping with a damp cloth; if necessary use a little rubbing alcohol to remove dirt.
○ All electrical equipment should be checked periodically to ensure that leads and connections are in good order.
○ Untwist the cord on the dryer from time to time.
○ Clean filters regularly – a blocked filter means the dryer has to work harder and will eventually overheat and cut out. If the element overheats it can distort the dryer casing.

BLOW-DRYING

By following our step-by-step
you can achieve the
smoothest, sleekest
blow-dry ever.

1 Shampoo and condition your hair.

5 Using your other hand, spread the mousse through the hair, distributing it evenly from the tips to the ends.

STYLING CHECKLIST

You will need:
✔ styling comb
✔ dryer
✔ mousse
✔ clip
✔ styling brush
✔ serum

2 Comb through with a wide-toothed comb to remove any tangles.

6 Divide your hair into two main sections by clipping the top and sides out of the way. Then, working on the hair that is left free and taking one small section at a time, hold the dryer in one hand and a styling brush in the other. Place the brush underneath the first section of hair, positioning it at the roots. Keeping the tension on the hair taut (but without undue stress), move the brush down towards the ends, directing the air flow from the dryer so that it follows the downwards movement of the brush.

3 Partially dry your hair to remove excess moisture.

7 Curve the brush under at the ends to achieve a slight bend. Concentrate on drying the root area first, repeatedly introducing the brush to the roots once it has moved down the length of the hair. Continue the movement until the first section of the hair is dry. Repeat step 6 until the whole of the back section is completely dry.

4 Apply a handful of mousse to the palm of your hand.

8 Release a section of hair from the top and dry it in the same manner. Continue in this way until you have dried all your hair. Finish by smoothing a few drops of serum through the hair to flatten any flyaway ends.

TIPS
○ Use the highest heat or speed setting to remove excess moisture, then switch to medium to finish drying.
○ Point the air flow downwards. This smoothes the cuticles and makes the hair shine.
○ When blow-drying, make sure each section is completely dry before going on to the next.

FINGER DRYING

This is a quick method of drying and styling your hair. It relies on the heat released from your hands rather than the heat from a dryer. Finger drying is suitable for short to mid-length hair.

1 Shampoo and condition your hair, then spray with gel and comb through.

> **TIP**
> Finger-drying is the best way to dry damaged hair, or to encourage waves in naturally curly, short hair.

2 Run your fingers rapidly upwards and forwards, from the roots to the ends.

> **STYLING CHECKLIST**
>
> *You will need:*
> ✔ spray gel
> ✔ styling comb

3 Lift up the hair at the crown to get height at the roots.

4 Continue lifting as the hair dries. Use your fingertips to flatten the hair at the sides.

BARREL CURLS

One of the simplest sets is achieved by curling the hair around the fingers and then pinning the curl in place. Barrel curls create a soft set.

1 Shampoo and condition your hair; apply setting lotion and comb through from the roots to the ends. Take a small section of hair (about 1 in) and smooth it upwards.

2 Loop the hair into a large curl.

3 Clip in place.

4 Continue to curl the rest of the hair in the same way.

5 Dry the hair with a hood dryer or allow it to dry naturally. Remove the clips. To achieve a tousled look rake your fingers through your hair. For a smoother finish use a hair brush.

STYLING CHECKLIST

You will need:
✔ setting lotion
✔ styling comb
✔ clips
✔ hood dryer (optional)

ROLL-UP

A roller set forms the basis of many styles; it can be used to smooth hair, add waves or soft curls, or provide a foundation for an upswept style.

TIPS

❍ Use large diameter rollers for sleek, wavy looks, smaller rollers for curlier styles.
❍ Always use sections of equal width when setting the hair or you will get an uneven result.
❍ For maximum volume and control, let the hair cool completely before brushing through.
❍ A bristle brush will give a smoother finish to the style.
❍ If the finished set is too curly after brushing through, loosen the curl with a brush used with a hand dryer.
❍ To create extra volume and height use a fine-toothed comb to backcomb the roots.

1 Shampoo and condition your hair, then partially dry to remove excess moisture. Mist with a styling spray.

2 For a basic set, take a 2 in section of hair (or a section the same width as your roller) from the center front and comb it straight up, smoothing out any tangles.

3 Wrap the ends of the sectioned hair around the roller, taking care not to buckle the hair. Then wind the roller down firmly, towards the scalp, keeping the tension even.

4 Keep winding until the roller sits on the roots of the hair. Self-fixing rollers will stay in place on their own but if you are using brush rollers you will have to fasten them with a pin.

5 Continue around the whole head, always taking the same width of hair. Re-mist the hair with styling spray if it begins to dry out.

6 Leave the finished set to dry naturally, or dry it with a diffuser attachment on your hand dryer, or with a hood dryer. When using artificial heat sources allow the completely dry hair to become quite cool before you remove the rollers. Brush through the hair following the direction of the set. Mist the brush with hairspray and use to smooth any stray hairs.

SOFT SETTING

Fabric rollers are the
modern version of old-
fashioned rags. Apart from
being very easy to use they are
kind to the hair and give a
highly effective set.

1 Dampen the hair with styling spray,
making sure you distribute it evenly
from the roots to the ends.

5 Leave the completed set to dry
naturally.

TIP
For even more volume, twist each
section of hair lengthwise before
winding it into the fabric roller.

2 Using sections of hair about 1 in wide, curl the end of the hair around a fabric roller and wind the roller down towards the scalp, taking care not to buckle the ends of the hair.

3 Continue winding the roller right down to the roots.

4 To fasten, simply bend each end of the fabric roller towards the center. This grips the hair and holds it in place.

6 When the hair is dry, remove the rollers by unbending the ends and unwinding the hair.

7 When all the rollers have been removed the hair falls into firm corkscrew curls.

8 Working on one curl at a time, rake your fingers through the hair, teasing out each curl. The result will be a full, voluminous finish.

STYLE AND GO

Hot brushes with tong attachments enable you to create lots of styles. Here we show you two different techniques, which give two different looks.

STYLING CHECKLIST

You will need:
✔ hot brush with tong attachment
✔ styling lotion

1 Shampoo, condition, and dry your hair.

2 Take a section of hair about 2 in square, and apply some styling lotion. Using the brush attachment gently smooth the hair from the roots to the ends. Place the hot brush near the roots, twist the hair around the brush, and hold for a few seconds. Gently unravel the hair and hold without pulling.

3 Place the ends of the hair into the hot brush and wind halfway down the hair length.

4 Unwind and loop the hair into a barrel curl, securing with a clip. Repeat steps 2 to 4 until you have done the whole head. Remove the pins. Comb.

1 Shampoo, condition, and dry your hair.

3 Continue wrapping the hair down the length of the barrel, taking care not to buckle the ends of the hair. Hold for a few seconds to allow the curl to form.

4 Release the depressor and allow the spiral curl to spring out. Repeat steps 2 to 3 until you have curled the whole head, then rake through the hair with your fingers for a softly tousled look.

Use the tong attachment for a tousled look.

2 Take a section of hair about ½ in long and apply some styling lotion. Using the tong attachment on the styler, lift the depressor and keep it open. Slide the tongs on to the hair, just up from the roots. Holding the depressor open, wind the hair around the barrel, towards the face, ensuring the ends are smooth.

TIP
After tonging the hair, don't be tempted to brush your hair or you will lose the curl.

STYLING TRICKS
❍ Always use heated hot brushes on dry hair, never on wet hair.
❍ Don't use mousse or gel when heat styling. Instead, try special heat-activated styling lotions and sprays. These are designed to help curls hold their shape without making the hair sticky or frizzy.
❍ Bobbed styles can be smoothed down and the ends of the hair tipped under using a hot brush. Just section the hair and smooth the tongs down the length, curving the ends. It is important to keep the tongs moving with a gentle sliding action, twisting the wrist and turning the barrel of the tongs under.
❍ Unruly bangs can be tamed by gently winding the bangs around the tong or brush and holding for a few seconds.

Hair by Keith Harris using Braun styling appliances, Photography Iain Phillpott

TONG AND TWIST

Tongs can also be used to smooth the hair and add just the right amount of movement.

1 Shampoo, condition, and dry your hair. Apply a mist of styling lotion. Never use mousse as it will stick to the tongs and bake into the hair. Divide off a small section of hair.

STYLING CHECKLIST

You will need:
✔ styling lotion
✔ tongs

2 Press the depressor to open the tongs.

3 Wind the section of hair around the barrel of the tongs.

4 Release the depressor to hold the hair in place and wait a few seconds for the curl to form. Remove the tongs and leave the hair to cool while you work on the rest of the hair. Style by raking through with your fingers.

TIP
Never use tongs on bleached hair. The high heat can damage the hair, causing brittleness and breakage.

AIRWAVES

Air waving makes use of gentle heat and combines it with the moisture in your hair to give a long lasting curl.

1 Shampoo and condition your hair. Mist with styling lotion.

3 Clip on the tong attachment and continue shaping the hair by wrapping it around the tongs.

4 Repeat steps 2 and 3 until the whole head is curled and waved. When the hair is completely dry rake your fingers through it.

2 Using the brush attachment on the styler, start drying the hair. Lift each section to allow the heat to dry the roots.

STYLING CHECKLIST

You will need:
✔ styling lotion
✔ electric air waver with brush and tong attachments

TIP
Switch your air waver to low speed for more controlled styling and finishing.

CURL CREATION

STYLING CHECKLIST

You will need:
✔ curl revitaliser
✔ wide-toothed comb
✔ dryer with pronged
diffuser attachment

A perm that is past its best
can be revived using this
diffuser drying technique.

1 The hair has the remains of a perm
and is therefore flat at the roots with
some curl from the mid-lengths to the
ends.

2 Wash, condition, and towel dry your hair, then apply curl revitalizer to the damp hair.

3 Use a wide-toothed comb and work from the roots to the ends to ensure the curl revitalizer is distributed evenly.

4 Attach the diffuser to the dryer and dry the hair, allowing the hair to sit on the prongs of the diffuser. This action enables the warm air to circulate around the strands of hair, which encourages the formation of curls. To maximize the amount of curl, use your hands to "scrunch" up handfuls of hair.

5 Tip your head forwards, allowing the hair to sit in the diffuser cup. Do not pull the hair, simply squeeze curls gently into shape.

6 Repeat steps 4 and 5 until all the hair is dry.

TIP
This technique works equally well on naturally wavy or curly hair, giving separation and definition to curls and waves.

Hair by Trevor Sorbie, London.

SMOOTH AND STRAIGHT

Volume can be added to long straight hair by using a dryer with a diffuser attachment that has long straight prongs.

1 Long thick hair often tangles easily and it is difficult to add volume and control.

2 Shampoo and condition your hair, then part it down the center. Attach a diffuser with long prongs to your dryer and, as the hair dries, comb the prongs down the hair in a stroking movement. This will direct the airflow downwards, smoothing and separating the hair.

3 To create volume at the top and sides, slide the prongs through the hair to the roots at the crown, then gently rotate the diffuser. Repeat until you have achieved maximum volume.

Photograph courtesy of Braun. Appliance, Braun Supervolume.

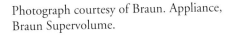

INSTANT SET

Hair can be given lift, bounce, and movement with a quick set using heated rollers.

1 Shampoo and condition your hair. Apply mousse and blow-dry smooth. Heat the rollers according to the manufacturer's directions.

2 Wind sections of hair (about 2 in wide) on to a roller, taking care not to buckle the ends of the hair. Use medium and small rollers at the front and sides, larger rollers on the crown.

STYLING CHECKLIST

You will need:
✔ mousse
✔ styling lotion
✔ heated rollers with clips

TIP
A heated roller set forms the foundation for many styles and is a simple way to restyle the hair

3 Wind the rollers down towards the root, making sure that the ends are tucked under smoothly. Keep the tension even. Secure each roller with the clip supplied. Mist your set hair with a styling lotion. Allow the rollers to cool completely and then remove them, taking care not to disturb the curl too much. To finish, loosen the curls by raking your fingers through them.

Hair by Trevor Sorbie, London.

CRIMPING CRAZY

If you use a crimper with a choice of styling plates you can devise a variety of looks that add instant ripples and waves to your hair.

1 This first step forms the basis for all the crimping styles. Before you begin, shampoo and condition your hair, then blow-dry it straight and mist with a styling lotion. Fit the styling plate of your choice to the crimper, following the manufacturer's directions. Working on one section of hair at a time, hold the hot crimper on your hair for a few seconds and then release. Move down the hair and apply the crimper again. Make sure that you line up the crimping plates carefully to ensure a uniform effect. Repeat to the end of the section of hair, then work around your head in the same way.

Left: For this crimped style, use the wave-making plates over the whole head.

All hairstyles on these two pages by Charles Worthington for BaByliss.

2 Use the standard crimping plates to give texture and volume to your hair, then section off the top hair into a ponytail and slip two bun rings over it. Finally, fan out random sections of hair and hold with firm-hold hairspray for a fun look.

3 Create a shimmer by using a crimping plate with a fine ridge. This not only adds texture to the hair, but also makes the hair look more shiny. Simply crimp the top sections of your hair at random. The effect can be used on long hair or hair cut in a bob.

4 For a slightly softer crimp, after shampooing and conditioning work some gel mousse through your hair before you dry it. This will help give it body. Then use the deep wave plates to create waves. Finally. ruffle through your hair using a wide-toothed comb to add more volume and softness.

TIP
❍ Don't use crimpers on bleached hair as the high heat needed to crimp the hair can cause drying and splitting.

5 Achieve this "bamboo" effect by crimping the hair in fine sections to produce a very crisp, definite effect. Starting from the roots, crimp down a section at a time, working as evenly as possible. When you have finished leave the hair in crimped sections, do not brush it through. Finally, secure a bun ring to the top of the head and grip the hair on to it in swirls, leaving a few lengths of hair sweeping down at the front to soften the style.

MEET THE EXPERT

International stylist Trevor Sorbie uses scrunching and other techniques to create these award-winning looks. His favorite tip is: "Let your fingers do the styling."

Thick, wavy hair like this model's tends to go frizzy and dull if left to dry naturally. Follow Trevor Sorbie's step-by-step guide to produce these beautiful results.

STYLING CHECKLIST

You will need:
For scrunching:
✔ styling spray
✔ section grips
✔ dryer with diffuser attachment
For fingerwaving:
✔ sculpting gel
✔ styling comb

1 Brush the hair off the face and then push the front hair forwards into waves. Secure the waves with a row of section clips and then apply a curl forming spray.

2 Use the diffuser attachment on your dryer to gently lift the curls. Dry the roots from underneath first, to help encourage lift and volume. When the hair is completely dry run your fingers through the hair to give definition. For extra texture and separation use a little soft wax, rubbing it between the palms of your hands first to warm it, then apply it to the ends of the curls with your fingertips.

To create a completely different look the hair is skilfully styled using finger waving techniques.

1 Shampoo and condition your hair. Towel dry to remove excess moisture, then apply a small amount of sculpting gel. Don't apply the gel directly from the bottle: dispense some on to the palm of your hand first.

2 Spread the gel on to the hair a little at a time, using your other hand to sculpt the hair into waves.

3 Part the hair in the center, then comb down smooth from the temples, as shown. Leave the ends around the hairline to curl freely. Use a comb with widely spaced teeth to shape the hair into waves, using your fingers and comb to create S-shapes. Allow to dry naturally or, if you are in a hurry, use a flat diffuser, which dries without ruffling the hair.

HAIR DRESSING

ONCE YOU HAVE MASTERED THE BASIC HAIR SETTING AND DRYING TECHNIQUES YOU CAN USE THESE SKILLS AS THE FOUNDATION FOR DRESSING YOUR HAIR IN MANY DIFFERENT STYLES. OUR SPECIAL PROJECTS SHOW YOU HOW TO CREATE BRAIDS, CHIGNONS, FRENCH PLEATS, TOP KNOTS, TWISTS, COILS, AND CURLS. BY FOLLOWING THE SIMPLE STEP-BY-STEP GUIDES, YOU CAN RECREATE THE LOOKS EXACTLY. YOU'LL BE AMAZED HOW EASY IT IS TO TOTALLY TRANSFORM YOUR HAIR TO SUIT ALMOST EVERY MOOD AND OCCASION.

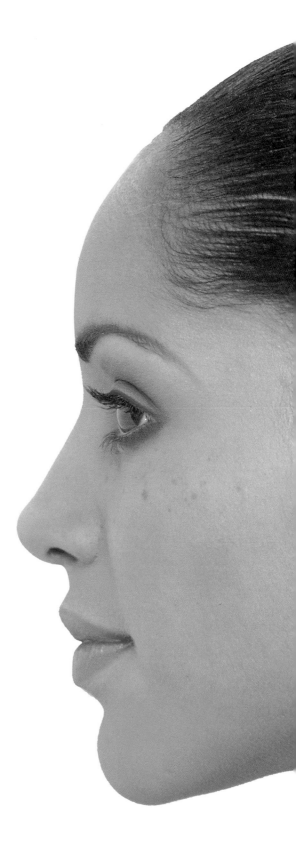

TWIST AND BRAID

Add interest to a classic style by twisting the sides of the hair and then weaving them into a braid.

1 Take a small section of hair on one side of your head, just above your ear, and divide it into two equal strands. Start twisting the two strands of hair together. Continue twisting downwards, towards the ends of the hair.

2 Secure the twist with a hair grip at the nape of the neck, then repeat these three steps on the other side.

3 Next, incorporate the twisted sections into a basic three-stranded braid. To braid, simply split the hair into three equal strands, taking the twisted sections into the left and right strands. Then bring the right strand over the center strand, the left stand over the center, and then the right over the center again. Continue in this manner to the end. Finally, secure the end with a covered band and decorate with a clip bow.

TIP
Smooth any stray ends of hair with a fine mist of hairspray.

DRAGGED SIDE BRAIDS

Curly hair can be controlled, yet still allowed to flow free, by braiding at the sides and allowing the hair at the back to fall in a mass of curls.

1 Part your hair in the center and divide off a large section at the side, combing it as flat as possible to the head.

2 Divide the section into three equal strands and hold them apart.

3 Begin to make a dragged braid by pulling the strands of hair towards your face and then braiding in the normal way, that is, taking the right strand over the center strand, the left strand over the center, and the right over the center again, keeping the braid in the position shown.

4 Continue braiding to the end and secure the end with a covered band. Tuck the braid behind your ear and grip it in place, then make a second braid on the other side.

TIP
Encourage curls to form by spraying the hair with water and then scrunching with your hands.

STYLING CHECKLIST

Time: 5 minutes
Ease/difficulty: Easy
Hair type: Long and naturally curly or permed

You will need:
✔ styling comb
✔ covered bands
✔ hair grips

PRETTY BRAID

Straight hair is smoothed to perfection, then enhanced with a tiny braided bow.

1 Part your hair in the center and, taking one section of hair at a time, run straightening irons from the roots to the tips to smooth out any kinks.

2 On one side of the head, midway along the center parting, pick up a small section of hair and comb it straight. Divide this section into three strands and braid the hair.

3 Continue in this way to the end, and then secure with a small covered band. Make a second braid on the other side of your head.

4 Finally, tie the braids in a bow at the center back of your head, as shown. Secure with pins and decorate the ends by binding them with fine ribbon.

STYLING CHECKLIST

Time: 10 minutes
Ease/difficulty: Quite easy
Hair type: Long, slightly wavy, or straight

You will need:
✔ straightening irons
✔ styling comb
✔ small covered bands
✔ short length of fine ribbon

RIBBON BOW

A simple ponytail is given added interest by binding with ribbon and finishing with a bow.

1 Brush your hair smoothly back into a neat ponytail, leaving a small section at either side free. Secure the ponytail with a covered band.

2 Position the center of the ribbon over the band as shown, pulling the ends of the ribbon taut.

3 Cross the ribbon over the ponytail.

4 Continue crossing the ribbon around the ponytail in the same manner until you are 2-3 in from the end. Tie the ribbon into a bow. Smooth out the side sections of hair and tie them into a neat bow at the center back of your head above the be-ribboned ponytail. Secure with a pin if necessary.

STYLING CHECKLIST

Time: 5 minutes
Ease/difficulty: Easy
Hair type: Long and straight

You will need:
✔ brush, comb
✔ covered band
✔ about 1 yd of ribbon

PONYTAIL STYLER

A simple ponytail can be transformed easily and quickly using this clever styler.

TIP
To smooth any flyaway ends rub a few drops of serum between the palms of your hands and smooth over the hair.

1 Clasp the hair into a ponytail and secure it with a covered band. Insert the styler as shown.

2 Thread the ponytail through the styler.

3 Begin to pull the styler down…

4 …continue pulling…

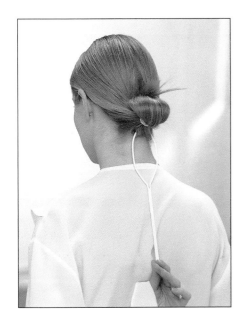

5 …so the ponytail pulls through…

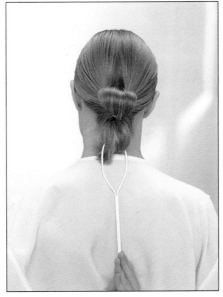

6 …and emerges underneath.

7 Smooth the hair with your hand and insert the styler again, repeating steps 2 to 6 once more to give a neat, chignon loop.

TIP
The same technique can be used on wet hair as long as you apply gel first, combing it through evenly before styling.

CURLY STYLER

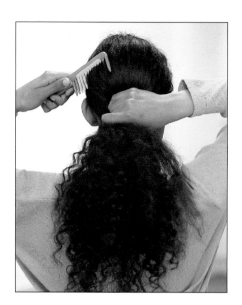

The ponytail styler can also be used to tame a mass of curls, creating a ponytail with a simple double twist.

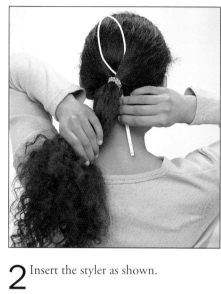

1 Use a comb with widely spaced teeth to smooth the hair back and into a ponytail. Secure with a covered band.

2 Insert the styler as shown.

3 Thread the ponytail through the styler.

Side view of finished style.

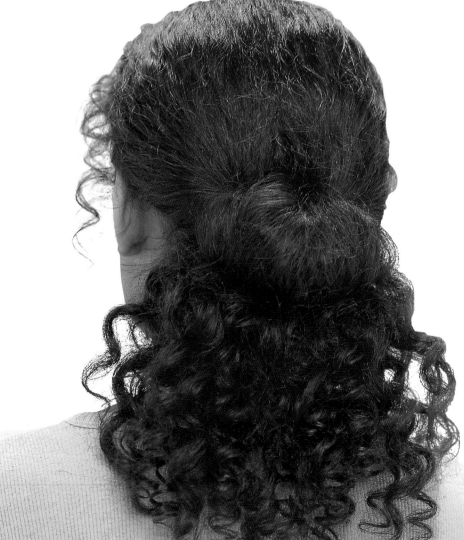

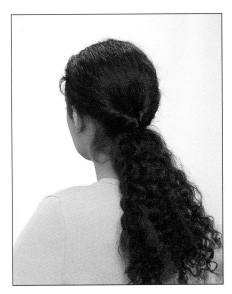

4 Begin to pull the styler down…

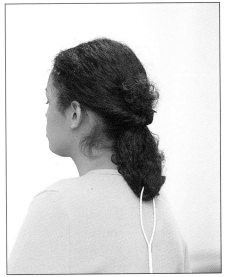

5 …continue pulling…

6 …so that the ponytail pulls through.

7 Repeat steps 3 to 6.

8 Apply a little mousse to your hands and use it to re-form the curls, scrunching to achieve a good shape.

STYLING CHECKLIST

Time: 5 minutes
Ease/difficulty: Easy
Hair type: Long and naturally curly or permed

You will need:
✔ widely spaced tooth comb
✔ covered band
✔ ponytail styler
✔ mousse

TIP
When inserting the styler through a pony tail, carefully move it from side to side in order to create enough room to pull the looped end of the styler through more easily.

FRENCH BRAID

This elegant, sophisticated braid looks complex but it does get easier with practice.

1 Take a section of hair from the front of the head and divide into three strands.

2 Braid once; that is, take the right strand over the center strand, the left over the center, and the right over the center.

3 Maintaining your hold on the braid with your fingers, use your thumbs to gather in additional hair (approximately ½ in strips) from each side of the head and add these to the original strands. Braid the strands once again.

4 Continue in this way, picking up more hair as you continue down the braid. Secure with a covered band and add an elastic ruffle.

TIP
Shorter front layers can be woven into this type of braid for example when growing out bangs.

STYLING CHECKLIST

Time: 5 minutes
Ease/difficulty: Quite difficult
Hair type: Mid-length to long and straight

You will need:
✔ covered band
✔ elastic ruffle

DOUBLE-STRANDED BRAIDS

These clever braids have a fishbone pattern, which gives an unusual look.

1 Part your hair in the center and comb it straight.

2 Divide the hair on one side of your hair into two strands, then take a fine section from the back of the back strand and take it over to join the front strand, as shown.

3 Now take a fine section from the front of the front strand and cross it over to the back strand. Take a fine section from the back strand again and bring it over to join the front strand. Continue in this way; you will soon see the fishbone effect appear. Secure the ends with covered bands and add feathers, tying in place with fine leather. Repeat these three steps on the other side.

TOP KNOT

Vary the look of finely braided locks by adding bright cord and tying the hair in a top knot.

1 Bind the end of each braid with cord, tying in a knot to secure.

2 Cross the braids over one another. Pick up and hold the braids from the crown section in either hand, as shown

3 Tie in a knot.

4 Repeat step 3 so you have a double knot. Secure the knot with a decorative hair pin.

STYLING CHECKLIST

Time: 15 -20 minutes
Ease/difficulty: Easy
Hair type: Long, finely braided or braided hair extensions

You will need:
✔ length of colorful cord about 5 yd long
✔ decorative hair pin

CROWN BRAIDS

By braiding the crown hair and allowing the remaining hair to frame the face you can achieve an interesting contrast of textures.

1 Clip up the top hair on one side of your head, leaving the back hair free. Take a small section of hair at ear level and comb it straight.

TIP
The volume of the curls can be increased by tipping your head forwards, then applying styling spray and scrunching the hair lying underneath.

2 Start braiding quite tightly, doing one cross (right strand over center, left over center), and gradual bring more hair into the outside strands.

3 Continue in this way, taking the braid towards the back of the head.

4 Make another parting about 1 in parallel to and above the previous braid, and repeat the process. Continue in this way until all the front hair has been braided. Scrunch the remaining hair into fulsome curls to increase the volume. Finally, add a decorative headband.

STYLING CHECKLIST

Time: 15 minutes
Ease/difficulty: Needs practice
Hair type: Mid-length to long and naturally curly or permed

You will need:
✔ large clip
✔ small covered bands
✔ headband

BASKET-WEAVE BRAID

STYLING CHECKLIST

Time: 10 minutes
Ease/difficulty: Needs practice
Hair type: Mid-length to long
and straight

You will need:
✔ styling comb
✔ elastic ruffle

You'll need to enlist the help of
a friend to help you create this
unusual braid.

1 Divide the hair into seven equal
strands – three strands on either side
of the face and one at the center back.

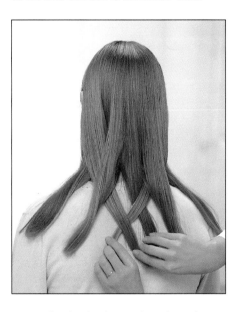

5 Take the third strand on the right-
hand side over the central strand, and
under the third strand on the left-
hand side.

2 Starting at the right hand side, cross the first strand (the strand nearest the face) over the second strand.

3 Cross the third strand over what is now the second strand, as shown.

4 Repeat steps 2 and 3 on the left side. What was originally the first strand in each group is now the third strand.

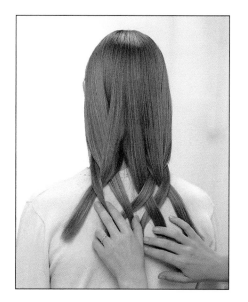

6 Now bring the first strand on the right-hand side over the second strand and under the central strand.

7 Repeat step 6 on the left side. Finally, clasp with an elastic ruffle.

DECORATED BRAIDS

Fine braids are quite time consuming to do, but they can be left in place for many weeks.

1 Take small sections of hair, about 1 in wide, and divide each section into three strands. Begin to braid.

STYLING CHECKLIST

Time: Depends on expertise, but even with practice it is time consuming
Ease/difficulty: Quite easy
Hair type: Works well on African-American hair

You will need:
✔ tiny covered bands
✔ about 5 yd of fine gold ribbon

2 Continue braiding from the roots down to the ends.

3 Secure the ends with a covered band and decorate with fine gold ribbon. Repeat all around the head.

TIP

If you are leaving braids in for more than a few days use a moisturizing spray to keep the scalp supple.

RICK-RACK BRAIDS

You can achieve a colorful style by braiding the hair with rick-rack to give a young, fresh style.

1 Braid the front of the hair as described on page 97. Tie three strands of rick-rack together at one end and pin to the covered band of one braid.

2 Take a section of hair and divide it into three strands, aligning one piece of rick-rack with each strand.

3 Begin braiding, taking the right strand over the center strand, the left over the center, right over the center, and so on.

4 Continue braiding down to the ends of the hair and tie the rick-rack to fasten.

STYLING CHECKLIST

Time: Time consuming
Ease/difficulty: Quite easy
Hair type: Naturally curly or permed

You will need:
✔ colored rick-rack (about 3-5 yd of each color)
✔ small covered bands

TWIST AND COIL

This style starts with a simple ponytail, is easy to do, and looks stunning.

1 Smooth the hair back and secure in a ponytail using a covered band.

2 Divide off a small section of hair and mist with shine spray for added gloss.

3 Holding the ends of a section, twist the hair until it rolls back on itself to form a coil.

4 Position the coil in a loop as shown and secure in place using hair pins. Continue in this manner until all the hair has been coiled. Decorate by intertwining with a strip of sequins.

STYLING CHECKLIST

Time: 10 minutes
Ease/difficulty: Easy
Hair type: Long, one length, straight hair

You will need:
✔ covered band
✔ pins
✔ hair pins
✔ shine spray
✔ 1 yd strip of sequins

CAMEO BRAID

A classic bun is given extra panache by encircling with a braid.

1 Smooth the hair into a ponytail, leaving one section of the hair free.

2 Place a bun ring over the ponytail.

3 Take approximately one third of the hair from the ponytail and wrap it around the bun ring, securing with pins. Repeat with the other two-thirds of hair.

4 Braid the section of hair that was left out of the ponytail, right strand over center strand, left over center and so on, and wrap the braid around the base of the bun, then secure with pins.

STYLING CHECKLIST

Time: 10 minutes.
Ease/difficulty: Needs practice
Hair type: Long and straight

You will need:
✔ covered band
✔ bun ring
✔ hair pins

ROPE BRAID

A simple braid is entwined with rope to give an unusual finish.

1 Divide off the top section of hair and comb it through. Hold in place with a clip and pin the rope in place on the crown.

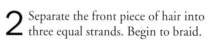

2 Separate the front piece of hair into three equal strands. Begin to braid.

3 When the braid reaches the top of the rope, merge a strand of rope with each strand of braid and continue working down to the ends.

4 Secure with a covered band. Make four more small braids, equally spaced around the head and secure the ends with small colored bands.

STYLING CHECKLIST

Time: 10 minutes
Ease/difficulty: Easy
Hair type: Long and straight

You will need:
✔ comb
✔ length of rope cut into equal pieces and tied at one end
✔ small covered bands

CITY SLICKER

Transform your hair in minutes using gel to slick it into shape and add sheen.

1 Take a generous amount of gel and apply it to the hair from the roots to the ends.

2 Use a vent brush, a comb, or your fingers to distribute the gel evenly through the hair.

3 Comb the hair into shape using a styling comb to encourage movement.

TIP
Make sure you distribute the gel evenly all over your hair before styling.

4 Shape to form a wave and sleek down the sides and back.

STYLING CHECKLIST

Time: 5 minutes
Ease/difficulty: Easy
Hair type: Short crops

You need:
✔ gel
✔ small vent brush
✔ styling comb

MINI BRAIDS

This young, fresh style is
perfect for teenagers.

2 Divide off a section at one side as shown and divide again into three equal parts.

1 Part the hair in the center and smooth with a little wax that has first been warmed between the palms of your hands before spreading over the hair.

3 Braid by placing the right strand over the center strand, the left over the center, right over the center, and so on, pulling the braid slightly towards the face.

5 Part the back hair into four equal sections, from the crown down to the nape, and braid as shown. This time, start the braid at the top with three strands of hair and, after each turn of the braid, add in a small section of hair from each side. The easiest way to do this is to lift up these additional sections of hair with your little fingers.

4 Continue down to the ends of the hair and secure with a small covered band. Repeat on the other side.

6 Secure the ends of the braids with small covered bands and decorate the braids with ribbon bows.

BAND BRAID

A plain ponytail can be transformed by simply covering the band with a tiny braid.

2 Divide this section into three equal strands. Now, braid the hair in the normal way.

1 Brush the hair back into a smooth, low ponytail, leaving a small section free for braiding. Smooth the reserved section with a little styling wax. Secure in place with a covered band.

3 Take the braid and wrap it around the covered band . . .

4 . . . as many times as it goes. Finally, secure with a grip.

CLIP UP

Long, curly hair can sometimes be unruly. Here's an easy way to tame tresses but still keep the beauty of the length.

1 Rub a little wax between the palms of your hands, then work into the curls with the fingertips. This helps give the curl separation and shine.

2 Take two interlocking large curved combs and use them to push the crown hair up towards the center.

3 Push the teeth of the combs together to fasten.

TIP
It's easier to disentangle curly hair if you use a comb with widely spaced teeth.

4 Repeat with two more combs at ear level to secure the back hair.

STYLING CHECKLIST

Time: 2 minutes
Ease/difficulty: Easy
Hair type: Mid-length to long, curly or straight

You will need:
✔ wax
✔ two sets of interlocking curved combs

DRAPED CHIGNON

This elegant style is perfect for that special evening out.

1 Part the hair in the center from the forehead to the middle of the crown. Comb the side hair and scoop the back hair into a low ponytail using a covered band.

2 Loosely braid the ponytail – take the right strand over the center strand, the left over the right, the right over the center, and so on, continuing to the end. Secure the end with a small band, then tuck the end under and around in a loop and secure with grips.

3 Pick up the hair on the left side and comb it in a curve back to the ponytail loop.

4 Swirl this hair over and under the loop and secure with grips. Repeat steps 3 and 4 on the right side.

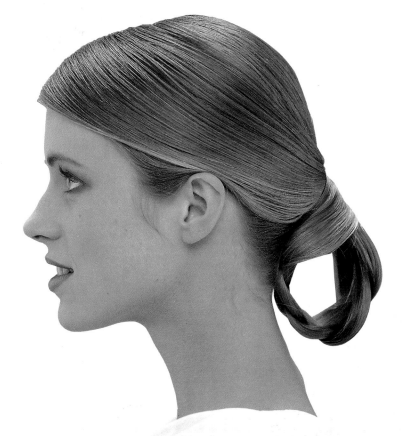

STYLING CHECKLIST

Time: 5-10 minutes
Ease/difficulty: Quite easy
Hair type: Long and straight

You will need:
✔ comb
✔ covered bands
✔ grips

TIP

Even long hair should be trimmed regularly, at least every two months, to keep it in good condition

UPSWEPT BRAIDS

Finely braided hair can be dressed up and decorated with sequins for a glamorous evening style.

1 Lift up the braids at the crown of the head and twist them around in one direction.

2 Secure in place with pins.

3 Gather up the remaining braids and loop them up to the crown.

TIP
Spray gloss misted over the braids will give a shine to the hair.

4 Pin in place and decorate by intertwining with sequins.

STYLING CHECKLIST

Time: 5-10 minutes
Ease/difficulty: Quite easy
Hair type: Long hair finely braided, or hair extensions

You will need:
✔ hair pins
✔ strip of fine sequins about 2 yd in all

SIMPLE PLEAT

Curly hair that is neatly pleated gives a sophisticated style. The front is left full to soften the effect.

1 Divide off a section of hair at the front and leave it free. Smooth with a little serum. Take the remaining hair into one hand, as if you were going to make a ponytail.

2 Twist the hair tightly from left to right.

3 When the twist is taut, turn the hair upwards as shown to form a pleat. Use your other hand to help smooth the pleat and at the same time neaten the top by tucking in the ends.

4 Secure the pleat with hair scroos or pins. Take the reserved front section, bring it back and secure it at the top of the pleat, allowing the ends to fall free.

STYLING CHECKLIST

Time: 5 minutes
Ease/difficulty: Quite easy
Hair type: Shoulder length or longer, curly or straight

You will need:
✔ serum
✔ hair scroos or pins

LOOPED CURLS

Two ponytails form the basis
of this elegant style.

3 Place the remaining hair in a lower
ponytail.

1 Apply setting lotion to the ends of the
hair only. This will give just the right
amount of body and bounce to help form
the curls. Set the hair on heated rollers.
When the rollers are quite cool – about 10
minutes after completing the set – take
them out and allow the hair to fall free.

2 Divide off the crown hair and secure
it with hair pins in a high ponytail.
Apply a few drops of serum to add gloss,
and brush the hair through.

4 Divide each ponytail into sections
about 1 in wide, then comb and
smooth each section into a looped curl
and pin in place. Set with hairspray.

STYLING CHECKLIST

Time: 10-15 minutes.
Ease/difficulty: Needs practice.
Hair type: Mid-length to long

You will need:
✔ setting lotion
✔ heated rollers
✔ serum
✔ covered bands, hair pins

FRENCH PLEAT

Mid-length to long hair can be transformed into a classic, elegant French pleat in a matter of minutes.

1 Backcomb the hair all over.

3 Gently smooth the hair around from the other side, leaving the front section free, and tuck the ends under.

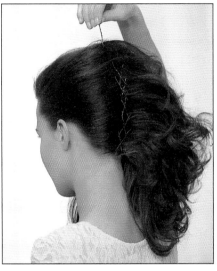

2 Smooth your hair across to the center back and form the center of the pleat by criss-crossing hair grips in a row from the crown downwards, as shown.

4 Secure with pins, then lightly comb the front section up and around to merge with the top of the pleat. Mist with hairspray to hold.

STYLING CHECKLIST

Time: 5-10 minutes.
Ease/difficulty: Quite easy
Hair type: Mid-length to long

You will need:
✔ comb
✔ hair grips
✔ pins
✔ hairspray

SHORT AND SPIKY

Short hair can be quickly styled using gel and wax to create a cheeky, fun look.

1 Work a generous amount of gel through your hair from the roots to the ends.

2 Dry your hair using a directional nozzle on your dryer; as you dry, lift sections of the hair to create height at the roots.

3 When the hair is dry, backcomb the crown to give additional height.

TIP
Gel can be re-activated by misting the hair with water and shaping it into style again.

4 To finish, rub a little wax between the palms of your hands, then apply it to the hair to give definition.

STYLING CHECKLIST

Time: 10 minutes
Ease/difficulty: Easy
Hair type: Short, layered and straight

You will need:
✔ gel
✔ blow-dryer
✔ comb
✔ wax

THE WEDDING

Short bobs look stunning worn
smooth and sleek and dressed
with a simple tiara.

1 Shampoo, condition, and partially
dry the hair to remove most of the
moisture.

2 Using a barrel brush attachment on an
airwaver, smooth the hair down section
by section to give a sleek finish. Add a pretty
tiara and adjust your make-up.

STYLING CHECKLIST

Time: 15 minutes after
shampooing and conditioning
Ease/difficulty: Easy
Hair type: Short, one-length bob

You will need:
✔ blow-dryer
✔ air waver
✔ tiara

1 Scrunch-dry your hair to create movement and volume.

2 Next curl the hair section by section, using a large barrel brush attachment on an air waver. This will smooth the curls and give an even fuller look. As each section is completed, pin it into a curl and leave to set until you have finished all the remaining hair. Remove the pins and brush through gently — curls and movement will spring into shape. Pin fresh flowers into the hair to add the finishing touch.

Hair: Denise McAdam, using Philips Haircare Appliances. Make-up: Jenny Jordan.
Photography Iain Philpott.

For a softer style, the hair is gently curled into romantic curls.

STYLING CHECKLIST

Time: 10-15 minutes after shampooing and conditioning
Ease/difficulty: Quite easy
Hair type: Short, one length bob

You will need:
✔ dryer with diffuser attachment
✔ air waver with large barrel brush attachment
✔ brush
✔ fresh flowers

COUNT DOWN TO THE BIG DAY

❍ Get your hair into condition with a series of intensive conditioning treatments.
❍ Once you have chosen your dress, experiment with different hairstyles. You might like to take photographs so you can compare the results before deciding which is the right style for you.
❍ Perms, highlights, or all-over color should be done about two weeks before the wedding. If you choose a longer-lasting semi-permanent, this can be done a week before.

Long hair is swept up into sophisticated curls.

1 Shampoo and condition your hair. Dry the hair using a medium heat setting on the dryer. The medium setting is gentle and easier on longer hair.

2 Put your hair up into a high ponytail and curl into loops, as described in step 4 on page 113. Pin in place. Curl short lengths of hair using an air waver fitted with a tong attachment. Just lift the depressor, wrap the hair around the barrel, hold for a few seconds, and then release the curl. Pin the tiara in place and attach the veil to the back of the head.

Hair: Denise McAdam using Philips Haircare Appliances. Make-up: Jenny Jordan.
Photography Iain Philpott.

STYLING CHECKLIST

Time: 10-15 minutes after shampooing and conditioning
Ease/difficulty: Needs practice
Hair type: Long and straight or naturally wavy

You will need:
✔ blow-dryer
✔ covered band
✔ pins
✔ air waver with tong attachment
✔ tiara
✔ veil

For a very feminine look the hair is delicately curled to fall in a mass of waves.

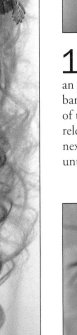

1 Shampoo, condition, and dry the hair. Fit the tong attachment on to an air waver and wrap the hair around the barrel, taking care not to buckle the ends of the hair. Hold for a few minutes, then release the curl. Pin it up and work on the next piece of hair. Continue in this way until you have tonged the whole head.

2 Release the curls and allow them to fall free. To give added separation and freedom to the curls, use a blow-dryer with a diffuser attachment. Set the dryer on a low heat/speed setting and gently ruffle the hair. This will increase the volume as well as separating the curls. To finish, clip back the hair and secure with a flower band.

STYLING CHECKLIST

Time: 20 minutes after shampooing and conditioning
Ease/difficulty: Needs practice

You will need:
✔ air waver with tong attachment
✔ blow-dryer with diffuser
✔ flower band

WIGS AND HAIRPIECES

Change your image in an instant with a wig or a hairpiece; it's a simple, quick, and effective way to change your looks.

The model, with her short urchin cut.

A classic *coupe sauvage* wig feathers on to the face.

All wigs and hairpieces by René of Paris, The Designer Wig Collection, Trendco, London.

Above: A wig styled in a short bob gives a neat head shape. *Left:* For instant length and glamor try a long blonde wig.

When adding hairpieces first slick the hair back into a tight ponytail, either high on the crown or at the nape, depending on the look you want to achieve.

Above: Two long hairpieces are used for this style. The first is attached to a low ponytail, twisted, and then pinned up. The second is coiled around to form a bun.

Above: Pre-curled hairpieces are clipped to a high ponytail, with some hair wound around and held with two elastic ruffles.

Two curly hairpieces are pinned to a high ponytail.

Braided hairpieces are coiled around to form a high chignon.

ACCESSORIES

Nothing becomes a hairstyle quite like hair accessories.
Bandeaux, ribbons, and bows come into their own at party time,
but they can also be used at any time to transform
your hair – instantly.

MAKE YOUR OWN

Some of the prettiest items for accessorizing the hair can be found in accessories departments of large stores. Look out for strips of sequins and pearls, or choose pretty ribbons and tiny embroidered flowers that can be tied or simply pinned into place.

ELASTIC RUFFLES

These are elasticized bands that are covered with a loose tube of fabric, which ruffles up when it is placed over a ponytail. They are available in a variety of fabrics including fine pleated silks and soft chiffons.

Left: An elastic ruffle completely alters the look of Twist and Coil (page 102).

BEADS

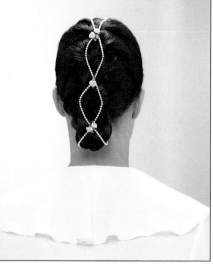

Above: The French Braid (page 94) is tucked up and decorated with a strip of tiny pearls and small fabric flowers.

Beads can be threaded on to strands of hair for special looks, and many accessories are, in fact, made of hundreds of small beads.

FLEXIBLE BANDS

Above: A flexible band used as a head band

Flexible bands are long pieces of wire encased in fabric – often velvet or silk – that can be twisted into the hair in a variety of eye-catching ways; for example as a band, braided into a ponytail, entwined round a bun, or bound on to a braid. They come in many different colors and materials.

BOWS

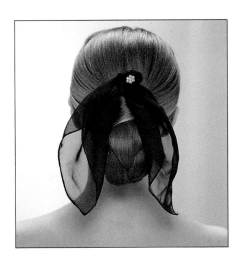

Above: A floppy bow adds instant sparkle to our Ponytail Styler (page 90).

Bows can be tailored or floppy, and are usually made from soft silks and velvets attached to a barrette.

FLOWERS

Above: Fresh flowers are pinned into the style Twist and Braid (page 86).

For special occasions, especially weddings, fresh flowers are perfect. However, if you want to keep your flowers afterwards use some of the beautiful silk alternatives.

HEADBANDS

Above: Add a beaded headband and an elastic ruffle to hair fixed in a low bun.

Headbands come in a wide variety of fabrics and widths. Classic colors such as black, navy, red, cream, and tortoiseshell are good basics.

BARRETTES, CHIGNON PINS, COMBS

Above: A pearl barrette gives added interest to Curly Styler (page 92).

Unusual fasteners and barrettes are excellent for finishing off a braid or adding interest to a ponytail. Chignon pins add instant sophistication and are a means of securing buns. Combs can be used to lift the hair off the face, allowing the hair to fall free, but not in your eyes.

Curly hair is versatile too, if you choose the right accessory.

Pin the hair back with jewelled slide clips.

Add elegance with a pearl-threaded covered band.

Pin artificial flowers on top of an upswept style.

For a very feminine touch add a pretty bow barrette…

…or an embroidered and bejeweled ribbon.

For the evening, clip a classic bow among the curls…

…or let the feathers fly.

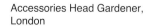

Left: Intertwine a gold and a black flexible band and use as a headband.

Accessories Head Gardener, London

Many of the styles created in the Techniques and Hair Dressing sections can be transformed in seconds by adding a pretty hair accessory.

Long straight hair can be dressed with a wide range of accessories to suit every occasion.

A classic snood with bow is used to gather up Decorated Braids (page 100).

The Cameo Braid (page 103) is transformed by the addition of a snood.

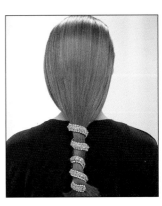

Try a pretty clip…

…or a simple beaded twist.

A black chiffon bow and a diamanté pin add another dimension to the Draped Chignon (page 110).

Simple but stunning: three chiffon scarves are braided and wound round a ponytail.

Make a ponytail, twist it and flip it up, then secure with a glittery band and three decorated clips.

This extravagant headband could double as a hat.

Left: Braids can be clipped up on to the crown and the ends clasped in an elastic ruffle.

Position flower bands down a length of ponytail…

…or use curved clips decorated with ribbons and a matching elastic ruffle.

Accessories Head Gardener, London

Flexible bands enable you to create a variety of styles.

Gather the top part of the hair into a ponytail and fit the band around in a twist. Make one cross with the band, then incorporate the lower hair into a braid. Squeeze the end of the band to secure.

For this style, simply fold the end of the hair and band under and press again.

Effect another transformation by bending the end up and securing it at the crown.

Put hair into a ponytail, then place one end of the band over to finish.

Accessories Head Gardener, London

Left: Fit the band around the head, cross the ends over to gather the hair into a ponytail, then bend the ends to finish as shown.

GLOSSARY

acid balanced having the same pH as the skin and hair, which is about 4.5.

anagen the stage in the life of a hair when the hair is actively growing.

backcomb to comb the hair from the ends down towards the roots.

bleach a chemical substance that removes the natural color from the hair.

blunt cut to cut the hair straight across at the ends.

bob short hairstyle created by blunt cutting.

camomile a low-growing aromatic herb. It is sometimes used to make shampoos and rinses for hair.

catagen a transitional stage in the life cycle of a hair between the stages of active growth and resting.

colorant a chemical substance that changes the color of the hair by masking the natural color. It can be temporary, semi-permanent, or permanent.

cortex the middle layer of a hair, which consists of bundles of fibers and contains the coloring matter melanin.

cuticle the outer layers of a hair, which protects the cortex.

dermal papilla the hair root.

dermis the innermost layer of the skin, which contains the hair follicle.

epidermis the outermost layer of the skin.

follicle a small depression in the skin that contains the hair root.

heat styling using heat by electrical appliances to style the hair.

keratin a protein that occurs in the outer layer of skin and is one of the main constituents of hair and nails. It consists of fibers containing sulfur.

medulla the innermost part of a hair.

melanin a dark brown or black pigment found in the hair, skin, and eyes.

movement a term applied to hair that, because of the cut, is able to move freely in all directions.

papilla *see* dermal papilla

pH a measurement of the acidity or alkalinity of a solution, read on a scale of 1 to 14. Solutions with a pH below 7 are acid; those with a pH above 7 are alkaline. A solution with a pH of 7.5 is neutral.

sebaceous gland a gland in the skin that produces sebum.

sebum an oily substance composed of waxes and fats that lubricates the skin and hair.

telogen a stage in the life cycle of a hair when growth stops completely; the resting stage.

trichologist a specialist who deals with hair and scalp problems.

INDEX

ADDITIONAL PICTURE CREDITS:
page 9 Edward Allwright; page 11
(scissors) Alistair Hughes;
pages 17, 19, 23 (above) Alistair
Hughes; page 23 (below) Michelle
Garrett; page 24 (top right) Mark
Gatehouse, (top left)
Bonieventure.